christmas cookbook

from the Cake Doctor

By Anne Byrn

at your service

Please direct comments or questions about *The Cake Mix Doctor Christmas Cookbook* to:

• Oxmoor House Special Editions
E-mail **SpecialEditions@spc.com** or write:
  Oxmoor House Special Editions
  2100 Lakeshore Drive
  Birmingham, AL 35209

• The Cake Mix Doctor
E-mail **anne@cakemixdoctor.com** or visit her Web site at **www.cakemixdoctor.com.**

Interested in more Oxmoor House books?
Find a wide variety of titles from your favorite brands— *Southern Living, Cooking Light,* Williams-Sonoma, and many more! Whether you enjoy cooking, gardening, or decorating, you'll find a wealth of how-to books that can be shipped straight to your door. Please visit **oxmoorhouse.com** for our many special offers, or call 1-800-765-6400.

The Cake Mix Doctor Christmas Cookbook is published by Oxmoor House, Inc., Book Division of Southern Progress Corporation, P.O. Box 2262, Birmingham, Alabama 35201-2262.
Copyright 2006 by Oxmoor House, Inc. No part of this publication may be reproduced in any form or by any means without the prior written permission of the publisher, excepting brief quotes in connection with reviews written specifcally for inclusion in a magazine or newspaper. Printed in the USA. All rights reserved. Recipes in the Christmas Cookbook are excerpted from The Cake Mix Doctor, Chocolate from the Cake Mix Doctor, Cupcakes from the Cake Mix Doctor, and The Dinner Doctor. Reprinted by permission from Workman Publishing Company, Inc.
ISBN-13: 978-0-8487-3202-8
ISBN-10: 0-8487-3202-2

christmas
cookbook
from the

Cake Doctor

EDITOR	Kelly Hooper Troiano
CONTRIBUTING DESIGNER	Amy R. Bickell
SENIOR COPY EDITOR	L. Amanda Owens
EDITORIAL ASSISTANT	Julie Boston
DIRECTOR, TEST KITCHENS	Elizabeth Tyler Austin
ASSISTANT DIRECTOR, TEST KITCHENS	Julie Christopher
FOOD STYLIST	Kelley Self Wilton
TEST KITCHENS STAFF	Nicole Lee Faber, Kathleen Royal Phillips, Catherine Crowell Steele, Ashley T. Strickland
PHOTOGRAPHY DIRECTOR	Jim Bathie
SENIOR PHOTO STYLIST	Kay E. Clarke
PHOTO STYLIST	Katherine Eckert
CONTRIBUTING PHOTOGRAPHERS	Billy Brown, Beau Gustafson, Lee Harrelson
CONTRIBUTING PHOTO STYLISTS	Lydia DeGaris-Pursell, Katie Stoddard
INTERNS	Jill Baughman, Jane Chambliss, Caroline Markunas, Lucas Whittington

OXMOOR HOUSE, INC.

EDITOR IN CHIEF	Nancy Fitzpatrick Wyatt
EXECUTIVE EDITOR	Susan Carlisle Payne
COPY CHIEF	Allison Long Lowery
VP, PUBLISHER	Brian Carnahan
DIRECTOR OF PRODUCTION	Laura Lockhart
SENIOR PRODUCTION MANAGER	Greg A. Amason
PRODUCTION ASSISTANT	Faye Porter Bonner

CROSSMAN LITERARY AGENCY

PRESIDENT	Nancy Crossman

SOUTHERN PROGRESS CORPORATION

PRESIDENT AND CEO	Tom Angelillo
EXECUTIVE VICE PRESIDENTS	Bruce Akin, Jeanetta Keller, Scott Sheppard
VP, ADMINISTRATION	Lane Schmitt
VP, CONSUMER MARKETING	John H. McIntosh, Jr.
VP, FINANCE	Bruce Larson
VP, PRODUCTION	Randy Lavies

Cover and at left: Chocolate-Almond Fudge Torte, page 89
Back cover: Holiday Yule Log, page 20; Countdown to Christmas Dinner menu, page 9; Snowman Cupcakes, page 34; Pumpkin-Orange Soup with Parmesan Toasts, page 71

Holiday Greetings
from Anne

Dear Busy Friend,

Maybe snow hasn't fallen and the wreath isn't on the front door, but in your heart it's already Christmas. We never outgrow the wonder of the season: the excitement in the air; the buttery, enticing aromas wafting from the kitchen; the familiar carols we sing with family; and the magical sight of presents under the tree. A joyful season awaits children of all ages!

Yet pulling off a picture-perfect holiday takes planning. If you're thinking ahead to Christmas with both excitement *and* trepidation, well relax, because the doctor is in! I'll help you plan menus, shop for parties, and cook for guests in my signature delicious and time-shaving style.

I wrote *The Cake Mix Doctor* nearly seven years ago; *Chocolate from the Cake Mix Doctor, The Dinner Doctor,* and *Cupcakes from the Cake Mix Doctor* followed. What I learned along the way is that no matter how busy we become, we still want to create wonderful meals for family and friends. And we search for recipes to call our own—even if they begin with a shortcut, such as a pre-roasted chicken or cake mix.

In *The Cake Mix Doctor Christmas Cookbook,* I share menus to enjoy during the holiday hustle and bustle, including a brunch for out-of-town guests, an elegant sit-down dinner, and mid-week family-style meals. Then I offer recipes that taste delicious and don't take all day to prepare. I also share tips and ideas to make meals more enjoyable and less stressful.

- **DISCOVER APPETIZERS,** such as Pecan Cheese Patties and Baked Vidalia Onion Dip (both on page 46), that will have your holiday guests begging for the recipes, plus a buffet that features an array of mouthwatering appetizers (page 14).

- **MAKE FAST, FRIENDLY RECIPES KIDS LOVE,** such as Spaghetti Casserole (page 57), Mom's Broccoli and Rice Casserole (page 68), and Creamy Scalloped Potatoes (page 66). If the kids are happy during this merry season, then so are you!

- **TOO BUSY TO FOLLOW A RECIPE?** Then check out one of my lists of 15 ideas for transforming deli hors d'oeuvres (page 83), frozen peas (page 67), and frozen mashed potatoes (page 68).

- **TURN TO MAKE-AHEAD HOLIDAY MENUS** that keep entertaining stress-free.

- **GET CREATIVE WITH GIFTS FROM THE KITCHEN**—they're the nicest presents to receive because they're made with love. You'll find Lemon-Pecan Biscotti and Easy Sweet and Hot Pickles (both on page 40).

- **BAKE DROP-DEAD GORGEOUS CAKES THAT BEGIN WITH A MIX.** Just dump, blend, and bake! Add a little from-scratch frosting and a simple garnish, and you'll have glorious holiday cakes, such as Christmas Cake Cones (page 33), Holiday Yule Logs (page 20), and Snowman Cupcakes (page 34).

- **DID I MENTION A FEW PERSONAL FAVORITES,** such as Chocolate-Almond Fudge Torte (page 89), as well as Caramel Cake and Italian Cream Cake (both on page 94)? I'm even sharing my best recipe for the holidays and year-round, too—The Best Pound Cake (page 97)—it's made with a yellow cake mix, but I promise that no one will ever know!

- **FOR WHEN CHRISTMAS DINNER IS A MERE MEMORY,** I include recipes for turning leftovers of turkey and ham into soups, salads, casseroles, and quesadillas (beginning on page 62).

Christmas is my favorite holiday because I adore making memories—and I can't wait to taste those special recipes we savor once a year.

Happy Cooking and Merry Christmas!

Anne

contents

Magical Moments   6

*Shortcut menus and recipes for holiday dinners
and gifts from your kitchen*

Holiday Cookbook   44

Easy recipes to mix and match all season long

Fast & Fabulous Finales   84

Quick fixes for spectacular desserts

magical moments

Discover shortcut menus and recipes for holiday dinners,

plus mouthwatering gifts from your kitchen.

Roast Pork Tenderloin with Fig and Chipotle Jam, French Green Beans Tossed with Fried Garlic, Souffléed Sweet Potatoes, and Angel Biscuits

Countdown to Christmas Dinner

It's the biggest holiday celebration of the year, and my streamlined recipes and handy timetable help you pull off the feast with ease.

Smoked Salmon Spread

(pictured on page 11)

SERVES: 6 to 8 (makes 1¼ cups)
PREPARATION TIME: 3 minutes

1 container (5.2 ounces) garlic-and-herb-flavored cheese spread
4 ounces sliced smoked salmon
1 tablespoon chopped fresh dill or chives
Pita triangles, crackers, and bagel chips, for serving

PLACE the cheese spread, smoked salmon, and dill in a food processor. Pulse 5 short times until the mixture is well combined. Spoon the spread into a serving bowl or onto a serving plate; surround it with pita triangles, crackers, and bagel chips and serve.

Roast Pork Tenderloin with Fig and Chipotle Jam

SERVES: 8
PREPARATION TIME: 15 minutes
BAKING TIME: 20 to 25 minutes
RESTING TIME: 10 minutes

1 cup fig jam or preserves
2 canned chipotle peppers in adobo sauce
2 pork tenderloins (1 pound each)
½ teaspoon salt
½ teaspoon black pepper
1 lime, cut into quarters

PLACE a rack in the center of the oven and preheat the oven to 425°F.
PLACE the fig preserves and the chipotle peppers in a food processor or blender and pulse until the mixture is smooth, 30 seconds. Set aside.
PLACE the pork tenderloins in a 13- by 9-inch (3-quart) glass or ceramic baking dish. Season the pork with salt and pepper. Spoon half of the jam mixture evenly over the top.
ROAST the pork until it browns, the juices run clear when pierced with a knife, and the meat is still barely pink, 20 to 25 minutes. Remove the baking dish from the oven, cover the meat with aluminum foil, and let it rest for 10 minutes.
SLICE the tenderloins and serve with the lime quarters and remaining half of the jam mixture.

Souffléed Sweet Potatoes

SERVES: 6 to 8
PREPARATION TIME: 15 minutes
BAKING TIME: 25 minutes

2 tablespoons (¼ stick) butter, plus 8 tablespoons (1 stick)
2 cans (29 ounces each) sweet potatoes in syrup, drained
¾ cup granulated sugar
⅔ cup all-purpose flour
¼ cup milk
2 large eggs

(continued on page 10)

Pork tenderloin is also delicious sliced and served cold the next day— that is, if any is left over!

---

menu

SERVES 6 TO 8

Smoked Salmon Spread

Roast Pork Tenderloin with Fig and Chipotle Jam

Souffléed Sweet Potatoes

French Green Beans Tossed with Fried Garlic

Southern Cranberry Salad

Angel Biscuits

Ambrosia Cake

timetable

1 TO 5 DAYS AHEAD
• Prepare Ambrosia Cake and store, covered, in the refrigerator.

1 DAY AHEAD
• Prepare salmon spread and salad. Store both in the refrigerator.

1½ HOURS AHEAD
• Mix together biscuits and cut with biscuit cutter. Cover until ready to bake.

• Prepare tenderloin and sweet potatoes and bake.

• While tenderloin and sweet potatoes bake, begin preparing green beans. Keep warm.

• While tenderloin rests, bake biscuits.

1 teaspoon grated orange zest
3 tablespoons fresh orange juice (from
    1 large orange)
1 cup pre-chopped pecans
1 cup firmly packed light brown sugar

PLACE a rack in the center of the oven and preheat the oven to 425°F.

PLACE the 2 tablespoons of butter in a 13- by 9-inch (3-quart) glass or ceramic baking dish and place the baking dish in the oven while it preheats.

MEANWHILE, place the sweet potatoes in a large mixing bowl and mash them with an electric mixer until smooth. There should be about 4 cups. Add the granulated sugar, ⅓ cup of the flour, milk, eggs, and orange zest and juice to the mashed sweet potatoes. Mix with an electric mixer on low speed until the ingredients are well combined and the mixture is smooth.

REMOVE the baking dish from the oven. Tilt the baking dish back and forth until the melted butter coats the bottom. Transfer the sweet potato mixture to the baking dish and spread it out evenly. Set it aside.

MELT the 8 tablespoons of butter in a small microwave-safe mixing bowl at high power for 45 seconds. Add the pecans, brown sugar, and the remaining ⅓ cup of flour; using a fork, stir until a crumbly mixture forms. Using the fork or your fingers, scatter the pecan topping evenly over the top of the sweet potatoes.

BAKE the sweet potatoes until they bubble around the edges and the pecans have turned golden brown, 25 minutes. Serve at once.

French Green Beans Tossed with Fried Garlic

SERVES: 6 to 8
PREPARATION TIME: 4 minutes
COOKING TIME: 8 minutes

2 tablespoons olive oil
2 tablespoons (¼ stick) butter
8 cloves garlic, chopped
¾ teaspoon salt
3 packages (9 ounces each) frozen
    French-cut green beans

PLACE the olive oil and butter in a small saucepan and heat over medium heat until the butter melts. Add the garlic and salt and cook, stirring, until the garlic browns, 3 to 4 minutes. Turn off the heat and set the pan aside.

PLACE the green beans in a medium-size glass bowl and heat in the microwave oven on high power for 5 minutes. Stir the beans, then continue cooking 4 minutes more until the beans are hot. Season the green beans with salt to taste, pour the garlic and oil mixture over them, and stir.

Southern Cranberry Salad

SERVES: 8
PREPARATION TIME: 10 minutes
CHILL TIME: at least 3 hours

1 package (3 ounces) strawberry or
    cherry gelatin
1 cup boiling water
1 can (16 ounces) whole-berry
    cranberry sauce
2 cans (11 ounces each) mandarin
    oranges, drained
1 can (8 ounces) crushed pineapple,
    drained
1 cup finely chopped toasted pecans
    (optional)
Lettuce leaves (optional)

PLACE the gelatin in a large heatproof glass or stainless steel bowl and pour the boiling water over it. Stir the gelatin with a fork until it has dissolved. Add the cranberry sauce, oranges, pineapple, and, if using, pecans and stir until well blended. Set the mixture aside.

LIGHTLY oil a 2-quart glass or ceramic baking dish or 4-cup ring mold. Transfer the cranberry salad to the baking dish or mold and cover the top with plastic wrap. Place the salad in the refrigerator and let it chill at least 3 hours, preferably overnight. The salad will take longer to set in ring mold than a baking dish.

TO SERVE, if using a baking dish, run a knife around the edges of the dish, cut the salad into servings, and, using a metal spatula, transfer them to a platter lined with lettuce leaves, if using. If using a ring mold, fill the sink with 1 inch of hot water. Let the ring mold sit in the water about 30 seconds. Run a sharp knife around the edges of the mold and then gently shake it to loosen the salad. Invert the mold onto a platter lined with lettuce leaves, if using.

Angel Biscuits

MAKES: 2 dozen
PREPARATION TIME: 19 minutes
BAKING TIME: 12 to 14 minutes

2 tablespoons very warm water
1 envelope (.25 ounce) rapid-rise dry
    yeast
3 tablespoons sugar
5 cups biscuit mix, such as Bisquick,
    plus more for dusting
½ cup solid vegetable shortening
1 cup buttermilk
2 tablespoons (¼ stick) butter,
    melted
Butter or preserves, for serving
    (optional)

Flaky like a biscuit, soft like a roll, sweet like a scone, these biscuits encompass the best of all worlds according to my children.

Smoked Salmon Spread (page 9)

PLACE a rack in the center of the oven and preheat the oven to 400°F.

PLACE the very warm water in a large mixing bowl, sprinkle the yeast over it, and stir until it dissolves. Add the sugar and stir until it dissolves. Add the 5 cups of biscuit mix and stir to combine well. Add the shortening and, using two dinner knives or a pastry cutter, cut the shortening into the mixture until well distributed and the mixture resembles peas. Pour in the buttermilk and stir with a fork until the ingredients come together.

DUST a clean work surface or large cutting board with biscuit mix. Turn the dough out onto the surface, dust your fingers with biscuit mix, and pat the dough out to flatten it. Flip the dough so that the floured side is up, then continue patting it with your fingertips until it is ¾-inch thick. With a lightly dusted 2-inch round biscuit cutter, stamp out biscuits and line them up closely on an ungreased baking sheet. As needed, collect the scraps of dough into a ball, knead the ball a few times, and press it out to a ¾-inch thickness, then stamp out more biscuits. Repeat until all of the dough has been used. Brush biscuit tops with melted butter.

BAKE the biscuits until they are light brown, 12 to 14 minutes. Remove the biscuits from the baking sheet and serve at once with butter and/or preserves if desired.

anne's tips

IF YOU HAVE ANY SALMON SPREAD LEFT OVER, though I don't predict this, here are some more yummy ways to enjoy it (they might even inspire you to make a double batch).

- Mix a tablespoon into an omelet.
- Spoon a tablespoon onto a baked potato instead of butter.
- Spoon tiny spoonfuls into hollowed-out cherry tomatoes—this is time-consuming, but worth it.
- Spoon the spread into large mushroom caps and bake them at 375°F until they are bubbling, about 15 minutes.
- Dollop a generous tablespoonful onto a portion of cooked pasta.
- Spread some onto a prebaked pizza crust and top it with cooked shrimp. Bake the pizza at 400°F until the spread is bubbling, 5 to 7 minutes.

Ambrosia Cake

Ambrosia Cake

SERVES: 16
PREPARATION TIME: 40 minutes
BAKING TIME: 15 to 17 minutes
ASSEMBLY TIME: 30 minutes

1 can (8 ounces) crushed pineapple in
    juice, drained
1 cup orange juice
1 cup sugar
Solid vegetable shortening, for
    greasing the pans
Flour, for dusting the pans
1 package (18.25 ounces) white
    cake mix

3 large eggs
1⅓ cups water
¼ cup vegetable oil
1 package (6 ounces) frozen grated
    coconut, thawed
Marshmallow Frosting
1¾ cups sweetened flaked coconut

COMBINE the pineapple, orange juice, and sugar in a 1½-quart saucepan. Cook over medium heat, stirring constantly, 20 to 25 minutes or until slightly thickened. Pour the filling into a bowl and cover with plastic wrap. Refrigerate the filling so that it will cool completely. Stir the filling before using it.

PLACE a rack in the center of the oven and preheat the oven to 350°F. Generously grease three 9-inch round cake pans with solid vegetable shortening, then dust with flour. Shake out the excess flour. Set the pans aside.

PLACE the cake mix, eggs, water, and oil in a large mixing bowl. Beat with an electric mixer at low speed 1 minute, stopping to scrape down the sides of the bowl with a rubber spatula. Increase the mixer speed to medium and beat 2 minutes or until blended and smooth. Fold in the grated coconut. Divide the batter among the prepared pans, smoothing it out with the spatula, and place the pans

I grew up learning that ambrosia is never more than coconut and oranges, but once I had it with crushed pineapple, I was inspired to create this sacrilegious rendition.

in the oven. If your oven is not large enough, place two pans on the center rack and place the third in the center of the highest rack.

BAKE the cakes until they spring back when lightly pressed with your finger and just start to pull away from the sides of the pans, 15 to 17 minutes. Be careful not to overbake the layer on the highest oven rack. Remove the pans from the oven and place them on wire racks to cool for 10 minutes. Run a dinner knife around the edge of the cakes and invert each onto a rack, then invert them again onto another rack so that the cakes are right side up. Allow them to cool completely. Meanwhile, prepare the Marshmallow Frosting.

PLACE one cake layer, right side up, on a serving platter. Spread the top of the cake layer with half of the filling, spreading the filling with a rubber spatula up to 1 inch from the cake edge. Place the second cake layer, right side up, on top of the filling. Spread the second layer with the remaining half of the filling, spreading it up to 1 inch from the cake edge. Top the two layers with the remaining cake layer, right side up, and spread frosting on the top and sides of the cake. Garnish the cake generously with the coconut, pressing it around the sides of the cake.

NOTE: Store this cake, covered in waxed paper or in a cake saver, in the refrigerator for up to 1 week.

Marshmallow Frosting

MAKES: 3½ cups
PREPARATION TIME: 7 minutes
COOK TIME: 4 minutes

½ cup sugar
2 tablespoons water
2 large egg whites
1 jar (7 ounces) marshmallow creme

PLACE the sugar, water, and egg whites in a 1½-quart saucepan. Cook over low heat, beating continuously with an electric hand mixer on high speed until soft peaks form, 3 to 4 minutes.

REMOVE the saucepan from the heat. Add the marshmallow creme and beat the mixture at high speed until stiff peaks form. Use at once to frost the cake.

15 ways to doctor canned cranberry sauce

1 Add grated fresh ginger and cardamom for an exotic punch to plain cranberry sauce.

2 Turn cranberry sauce into a chutney by adding a finely chopped shallot or onion, chopped dried figs, a couple tablespoons of vinegar, a little cinnamon, and some shelled pistachio nuts.

3 Fold in dried cherries.

4 Turn it into a lovely fruit salad with orange segments and chopped apple and/or pear. Add toasted pecans, if you like.

5 Make a warm fruit compote. Warm the sauce with canned pears, dried apricot pieces, and dried apple pieces. Add red wine and sugar to taste.

6 Fold in chopped fresh pineapple.

7 Make a red ambrosia with cranberry sauce, orange segments, and grated coconut.

8 Finish baked acorn or butternut squash with a spoonful of cranberry sauce, then warm thoroughly in the oven.

9 Blend it with prepared horseradish, chopped red onion, and sour cream for an interesting relish to serve with roasted beef.

10 Fold in toasted walnuts and pecans to turn it into an English conserve.

11 Blend it with mincemeat for an interesting pie filling or coffee cake topping.

12 Fold in chopped apples and add to your favorite baked pie crust. Top with whipped cream and a dusting of cinnamon.

13 Warm the sauce, adding a little melted butter and a bit of balsamic vinegar and red wine, and serve this as a sauce for duck or turkey.

14 Mix with orange marmalade and spread onto turkey or ham sandwiches.

15 Blend with cream cheese and fresh orange zest for a festive holiday morning bagel spread.

menu

Shrimp Cocktail Four Ways,
Pat's Mini Ham Biscuits, and
Red Pepper and Garlic Hummus

Easy, Breezy Appetizer Buffet

Friends will love to graze this festive assortment of make-ahead munchies fit for a meal.

Shrimp Cocktail Four Ways

SERVES: 12 to 15
PREPARATION TIME: 5 minutes per sauce

Mexican Cocktail Sauce

1 can (14.5 ounces) diced tomatoes
    with mild green chiles, with their
    liquid
1 small avocado, cut into ½-inch
    cubes (for ½ cup)
2 tablespoons chopped fresh
    cilantro
1 tablespoon fresh lime juice
½ teaspoon ground cumin,
    or more to taste
Drop of hot pepper sauce,
    or more to taste

American Cocktail Sauce

1 can (14.5 ounces) diced tomatoes
    with onions, with their liquid
1 tablespoon prepared horseradish
1 tablespoon fresh lemon juice
1 teaspoon Worcestershire sauce

Asian Cocktail Sauce

1 can (14.5 ounces) diced tomatoes,
    with their liquid
1 tablespoon hoisin sauce
1 tablespoon fresh lime juice
1 teaspoon peeled grated fresh ginger
    or pre-chopped ginger
½ teaspoon curry powder

Italian Cocktail Sauce

1 can (14.5 ounces) diced tomatoes
    with balsamic vinegar, basil, and
    olive oil, with their liquid
2 tablespoons chopped black olives
    (from 8 olives)
2 tablespoons chopped fresh flat-leaf
    parsley
1 tablespoon fresh lemon juice

2 pounds store-bought, peeled, deveined,
    and steamed large shrimp, thawed
    if frozen, and chilled

PLACE the ingredients for whichever sauce you are making in a medium-size glass bowl and stir to combine. Cover the sauce with plastic wrap and refrigerate until ready to serve.

PLACE the shrimp on a pretty platter in an attractive mound. If they still have their tails attached, these can be used to pick up the shrimp. If not, set out cocktail toothpicks. Spoon the sauce(s) of your choice into a serving bowl(s). And don't forget to set out plenty of napkins and forks for eating the chunkier sauces.

Pat's Mini Ham Biscuits

SERVES: 12 to 15
PREPARATION TIME: 20 minutes
BAKING TIME: 18 to 20 minutes

1 bag (25 ounces; 12 biscuits) frozen
    unbaked biscuits
12 ounces country ham slices, cooked,
    or 12 ounces pre-cooked sugar-
    cured ham
4 to 5 tablespoons mayonnaise
1 tablespoon finely minced onion or
    pickle relish
¼ cup all-purpose flour, for dusting

PREHEAT the oven to 375°F.
PLACE the frozen biscuits on an ungreased baking sheet and set them aside to thaw at room temperature while you prepare the ham.
TEAR the ham into pieces and place them in a food processor. Process until the ham is ground and crumbly, 10 seconds. Transfer the ham to a mixing bowl and stir in 4 tablespoons of the mayonnaise and either the onion or pickle relish. Add another tablespoon of mayonnaise if needed to bind the ham. Cover the bowl with plastic wrap and place it in the refrigerator while you cut out and bake the biscuits.
LIGHTLY dust a work surface with flour. When the biscuits are still cool to the touch but are soft enough to cut, place them on the lightly floured surface. Use a 1½-inch biscuit or round cookie cutter to cut each biscuit into three rounds. (You'll have to flatten out the dough after each cut to get three rounds from one biscuit.) Place the biscuit rounds on the baking sheet. Discard the scraps of dough. Bake the biscuits until golden brown, 18 to 20 minutes.
WHILE the biscuits bake, remove the ham salad from the refrigerator. When the biscuits are cool enough to handle, split them in half with a fork, spoon on 1 teaspoon of the ham mixture, and replace the tops. Place the filled biscuits on a serving tray; serve at once.

Red Pepper and Garlic Hummus

MAKES: 4 cups
PREPARATION TIME: 5 minutes

2 cups store-bought roasted red peppers,
    cut into strips (from 1 [24-ounce] jar)
4 cloves garlic, peeled
2 cans (15 ounces each) chickpeas,
    drained
¼ cup olive oil
2 teaspoons curry powder (optional)
Salt and black pepper
Pita crisps or soda crackers,
    for serving

PLACE the red pepper strips and garlic in a food processor and pulse quickly 7 or 8 times until pureed. Add the chickpeas, 1 tablespoon of the olive oil, and, if using, the curry powder. Process until pureed, about 30 seconds. Midway through, stop the machine and scrape down the sides of the bowl with a rubber spatula if needed. Season with salt and pepper to taste and add more olive oil if the puree is too dry. Using a rubber spatula, transfer the hummus to a serving bowl. Serve with pita crisps or crackers.

Devil's Food All-Stars

MAKES: 5 dozen
PREPARATION TIME: 20 minutes
BAKING TIME: 8 to 12 minutes
CHILL TIME: at least 3 hours

1 package (18.25 ounces) plain devil's
    food cake mix
12 tablespoons (1½ sticks) unsalted
    butter, at room temperature
1 large egg
1½ teaspoons pure vanilla extract
Flour, for rolling out the cookies
¼ cup turbinado sugar (optional)

PLACE the cake mix, butter, egg, and vanilla in a large mixing bowl. Blend with an electric mixer on low speed for 1 minute. The dough will be thick and will come together into a ball. Cover the bowl with plastic wrap and place it in the refrigerator to chill for at least 3 hours, or preferably overnight.
REMOVE dough from the refrigerator.

Dust a work surface with flour. Assemble your cookie cutters, a long metal spatula (to help transfer the cookie dough to the sheets), and a metal pancake spatula (for removing the cookies from the sheets).
PLACE a rack in the center of the oven and preheat the oven to 350°F. Set aside two ungreased cookie sheets.
WORKING with a quarter of the dough at a time and keeping the remaining dough in the refrigerator, place the dough on the floured surface and pound and roll it out to ¼-inch thickness. Cut the dough with a 2½-inch star-shaped cookie cutter and transfer them to the ungreased cookie sheets, using the long metal spatula. Sprinkle them with sugar. Place the cookie sheets in the oven. (If your oven cannot accommodate both cookie sheets on the center rack, place one on the top rack and one on the center rack and rotate them halfway through the baking time.)
BAKE the cookies until they puff up and

then sink back, 8 to 12 minutes. Remove the cookie sheets from the oven and let the cookies rest on the cookie sheets for 1 minute. Then use the spatula to transfer them to wire racks and allow them to cool completely and get crisp, 15 minutes.
REPEAT the rolling, cutting, and baking process with the remaining dough.

NOTE: Store these cookies, in a cake saver or in a metal tin, at room temperature for up to 1 week. Or freeze them, wrapped in foil, for up to 6 months. Thaw the cookies overnight on the counter before serving.

Pear and Blue Cheese Tartlets

MAKES: 30 tartlets
PREPARATION TIME: 10 minutes
BAKING TIME: 7 to 8 minutes

2 packages (2.1 ounces each) frozen
    miniature phyllo shells
1 tablespoon butter
2 pears, peeled and chopped
2 teaspoons sugar
1 wedge (5 ounces) Saga blue cheese,
    or another creamy blue, trimmed
    of rind and cut into 30 small cubes

PREHEAT the oven to 350°F.
PLACE the frozen phyllo shells on a rimmed baking sheet. Set the baking sheet aside.
MELT the butter in a small skillet over medium-high heat. Place the pears in the skillet and cook, stirring, for 1 minute to soften slightly. Sprinkle the sugar over the pears and cook, stirring, until they are completely soft, 2 minutes longer. Remove the skillet from the heat.
PLACE 1 teaspoon of the pears and their juice in each phyllo shell. Top with a cube of blue cheese.
BAKE the tartlets until the cheese melts and the shells are crisp and golden brown, 7 to 8 minutes. Remove the baking sheet from the oven and serve the tartlets immediately.

NOTE: The tartlets can be made up to 1 day in advance. Reheat them in an oven preheated to 350°F, 3 to 4 minutes.

Devil's Food All-Stars

Fresh Raspberry
Cream Cakes

Fresh Raspberry Cream Cakes

MAKES: 2 dozen
PREPARATION TIME: 35 minutes
FREEZING TIME: at least 3 hours

24 foil liners for cupcake pans
   (2½-inch size)
1½ cups graham cracker crumbs
½ cup finely chopped pecans
6 tablespoons (¾ stick) butter, melted
2 cups fresh raspberries, washed and
   drained (2 half-pint containers)
2 packages (8 ounces each) reduced-
   fat cream cheese, at room
   temperature
2 cans (14 ounces each) sweetened
   condensed milk
2 containers (8 ounces each) frozen
   whipped topping, thawed

Fresh Raspberry Cream Cakes
are tiny bites of heaven.

LINE 24 cupcake cups with the foil liners and set the pans aside.

PLACE the graham cracker crumbs, pecans, and melted butter in a mixing bowl and stir to combine. Spoon about 1 tablespoon of the mixture into each liner, pressing down on the mixture with your fingers to make the crust.

RESERVE 24 raspberries for garnish. Place the remaining raspberries in a food processor and pulse the berries until pureed, 10 seconds. Measure out ½ cup for the filling and set aside. Place the remaining puree in a sieve over a glass bowl to catch the juices. Push down gently on the puree to extract as much juice as possible. Discard the solids. Cover the raspberry juice with plastic wrap and refrigerate until needed.

PLACE the cream cheese in a large mixing bowl. Beat the cream cheese with an electric mixer on low speed until creamy, 30 seconds. Turn off the machine and add the sweetened condensed milk and the reserved ½ cup pureed raspberries. Blend with the mixer on medium speed until just combined, 20 to 60 seconds. Stop the mixer, add 2 cups of the whipped topping, and blend on low speed to combine, 15 seconds.

TOP the crusts with the raspberry mixture, dividing it evenly among them. The liners should be very full but not overflowing. Cover the pans with plastic wrap and place them in the freezer until firm, at least 3 hours.

REMOVE the pans from the freezer 15 minutes before serving. To serve the cakes, peel away the foil liners from the cakes and place the cakes on serving plates. Dollop each with a heaping tablespoonful of the remaining whipped topping; drizzle with the reserved raspberry juice and garnish with a reserved raspberry.

NOTE: Store these "cupcakes," ungarnished, covered with plastic wrap, in the freezer for up to 2 weeks.

Kathy's Cinnamon
Breakfast Cake

Memorable Desserts

Invite young family members into the kitchen to join in making favorite holiday desserts. These recipes teach basic cooking techniques using today's shortcut techniques.

Kathy's Cinnamon Breakfast Cake

SERVES: 16
PREPARATION TIME: 15 minutes
BAKING TIME: 58 to 60 minutes
ASSEMBLY TIME: 3 minutes

Vegetable oil cooking spray, for misting the pan
Flour, for dusting the pan
1/3 cup packed light brown sugar
2 teaspoons ground cinnamon
1/2 cup chopped pecans or walnuts
1 package (18.25 ounces) plain yellow cake mix
1 package (3.4 ounces) vanilla instant pudding mix
3/4 cup vegetable oil, such as canola, corn, safflower, soybean, or sunflower
3/4 cup water
4 large eggs
1 teaspoon pure vanilla extract
Glaze

PLACE a rack in the center of the oven and preheat the oven to 350°F. Lightly mist a 12-cup Bundt pan with vegetable oil cooking spray, then dust with flour. Shake out the excess flour.
FOR THE FILLING, place the brown sugar and cinnamon in a small bowl and stir until well combined. Set the bowl aside. Sprinkle the pecans in the bottom of the prepared pan. Set the pan aside.

PLACE the cake mix, pudding mix, oil, water, eggs, and vanilla in a large mixing bowl. Blend with an electric mixer on low speed for 1 minute. Stop the machine and scrape down the sides of the bowl with a rubber spatula. Increase the mixer speed to medium and beat 2 minutes more, scraping down the sides again if needed. The batter should look thick and smooth. Pour half of the batter into the prepared pan. Scatter all of the filling evenly over the batter. Pour the remaining batter evenly over the top, smoothing it out with the rubber spatula. Place the pan in the oven.
BAKE the cake until it is golden brown and springs back when lightly pressed with your finger, 58 to 60 minutes. Remove the pan from the oven and place it on a wire rack to cool for 20 minutes. Run a long, sharp knife around the edge of the cake and invert it onto a rack. Allow it to cool completely, 30 minutes more.
MEANWHILE, prepare the glaze.
WHEN the glaze is made, place the cooled cake on a serving platter and spoon the glaze over the top so that it drizzles down the sides and into the center of the cake. Slice and serve.

NOTE: Store this cake, covered in aluminum foil or under a glass cake dome, at room temperature for up to 1 week. Or freeze it, wrapped in foil, for up to 6 months. Thaw the cake overnight on the counter before serving.

Glaze

MAKES: 1/4 cup
PREPARATION TIME: 3 minutes

1 cup confectioners' sugar, sifted
2 tablespoons milk
1/2 teaspoon pure vanilla extract

PLACE the confectioners' sugar, milk, and vanilla in a small bowl and stir until smooth. Use immediately to glaze cake.

Chocolate Mocha Swirl Cheesecake Squares

SERVES: 20
PREPARATION TIME: 15 minutes
BAKING TIME: 35 to 40 minutes
CHILL TIME: at least 1 hour

Softened butter or solid vegetable shortening, for greasing the pan
1 package (18.25 ounces) plain devil's food cake mix
4 tablespoons (1/2 stick) butter, melted
4 large eggs
2 packages (8 ounces each) cream cheese, at room temperature
1 can (14 ounces) sweetened condensed milk
1/2 cup sour cream
2 teaspoons pure vanilla extract
1 tablespoon instant coffee powder
2 ounces semisweet or bittersweet chocolate, melted

PLACE a rack in the center of the oven and preheat the oven to 325°F. Lightly grease a 13- by 9-inch baking pan with softened butter or vegetable shortening. Set the pan aside.
MEASURE out 1/2 cup of the cake mix and set aside for the filling.
PLACE the remaining cake mix, the melted butter, and 1 egg in a large mixing bowl. Blend with an electric mixer on low speed for 2 minutes. Stop the machine and scrape down the sides of the bowl with a rubber spatula. The

(continued on page 20)

anne's tip

THE FILLING IN Kathy's Cinnamon Breakfast Cake is made of cinnamon and brown sugar. Simply pour half of the batter into the prepared pan and scatter all of the filling evenly over the batter. Smooth the remaining batter on top of the filling.

batter should come together in a ball. With your fingertips, pat the batter evenly over the bottom and 1 inch up the sides of the prepared pan, smoothing it out with your fingers until the top is smooth. Set the pan aside.

FOR THE FILLING, place the cream cheese and the sweetened condensed milk in the same mixing bowl that was used to make the crust and with the same beaters (no need to clean either) blend with an electric mixer on low speed until just combined, 30 seconds. Stop the machine and add the reserved cake mix, the remaining 3 eggs, the sour cream, vanilla, and coffee powder and beat on medium speed for 1 minute. Stop the machine and scrape down the sides of the bowl with a rubber spatula.

REMOVE 1 cup of the batter, place it in a small bowl, and whisk in the melted chocolate until the mixture is well combined. Set the chocolate mixture aside.

POUR the coffee-flavored filling onto the crust and spread with the rubber spatula so that the filling covers the entire surface and reaches the sides of the pan. With a tablespoon, drop chocolate mixture on top of the filling. With a dinner knife, swirl the chocolate mixture around in the batter to create a marbled effect (see tip and photo below). Place the pan in the oven.

BAKE the cheesecake until it looks shiny and the center no longer jiggles when you shake the pan, 35 to 40 minutes. Remove the pan from the oven and place it on a wire rack to cool, 30 minutes. Lightly cover the pan with plastic wrap and place the pan in the refrigerator to chill for at least 1 hour, but preferably 24 hours for the flavors to meld. Cut into squares and serve.

NOTE: Store cake, covered in plastic wrap or aluminum foil, in the refrigerator for up to 1 week. Or freeze it, wrapped in foil, for up to 2 months. Thaw the cake overnight in the refrigerator before serving.

Holiday Yule Logs

SERVES: 6 servings each for 2 filled rolls
PREPARATION TIME: 45 minutes
BAKING TIME: 13 minutes per roll
CHILL TIME: at least 1 hour

4 cups heavy (whipping) cream
2 cups confectioners' sugar, sifted
4 tablespoons brandy, or to taste
Vegetable oil cooking spray, for
    misting the pans
4 large eggs
½ cup water
1 package (18.25 ounces) devil's food
    cake mix
2 tablespoons unsweetened cocoa
    powder
Chocolate Ganache

PLACE a clean large mixing bowl and electric mixer beaters in the freezer for a few minutes while you assemble the ingredients for the whipped cream. Pour the heavy cream into the chilled bowl and beat with the electric mixer on high speed until the cream has thickened, 2 minutes. Stop the machine and add the sugar and half of the brandy. Beat the mixture on high for 30 seconds more, then add the remaining brandy to taste if desired. Beat until stiff peaks form, 1 to 2 minutes more. Cover the bowl with plastic wrap and place the filling in the refrigerator to chill.

PLACE a rack in the center of the oven and preheat the oven to 350°F. Mist the bottom of two 15- by 10-inch jelly-roll pans with vegetable oil cooking spray and cover with enough waxed paper to cover the bottom and still have a couple of inches lapping over at each end. Mist the waxed paper. Set the pans aside.

PLACE the eggs in a large mixing bowl. Blend with an electric mixer at medium-high for 5 minutes. Decrease the mixer speed to low and add the water. Gradually add the cake mix, beating until moistened. Increase the mixer speed to medium-high speed and beat for 2 minutes. Pour the batter into the prepared pans, smoothing it out with the rubber spatula. (Layers will be thin.) Place the pans in the oven.

BAKE the cakes until they spring back when lightly pressed with your finger, 13 minutes. (If you don't have a double oven, set one pan aside.) Remove the pans from the oven and place on wire racks. Dust a clean kitchen towel or long sheet of parchment paper with cocoa; repeat with a second towel. Immediately invert one pan onto each towel and carefully peel off the used waxed paper that clings to the bottom of the cakes. While the cakes are still hot, use the towel to help carefully roll each cake into a jelly roll, or roulade. Begin with the short side next to you and roll away from you. Place the roulades, seam sides down, wrapped in the kitchen towels or parchment paper, on the counter to cool completely.

MEANWHILE, prepare the Chocolate Ganache.

WHEN the ganache is made, the filling has chilled, and the cakes have cooled, you are ready to assemble the logs. Reserve 3 cups filling, covered, in the refrigerator. Carefully unroll the cakes just enough so that you can spread the inside surface generously with the chilled filling. Gently roll each cake back into the log shape, carefully pulling the kitchen towel out from under it. Place the logs, seam sides down, in front of you. Carefully cut off a 1-inch-thick slice from one end of each log.

CAREFULLY place each log, seam side down, on a serving platter. Place cut half of each log, cut side down, on the side of the log to resemble a knot on a branch and attach to the log with a dab of ganache. Working quickly, spread ganache over the entire surface of each log with clean strokes, covering the ends. Make the strokes irregular so that

anne's tip

THERE'S NO NEED TO FEEL NERVOUS about swirling the filling in Chocolate Mocha Swirl Cheesecake Squares. Use a dinner knife to make figure eights, zigzags, or wavy lines to create a marbled look. And don't worry about poking the crust by mistake. It's really pretty sturdy.

Holiday Yule Log

anne's tip

GENTLY REROLL THE CAKE LAYER for Holiday Yule Log back into its log shape once the surface has been spread with filling. Then carefully pull the kitchen towel out from under the log.

the ganache resembles the bark of a tree. Or drag a fork down through the ganache so that the tines of the fork make lines in the batter, also resembling bark. Place the platters in the refrigerator to chill until the ganache has set, 1 hour. Then, lightly cover the logs with waxed paper and chill until serving time.

SLICE into serving pieces and serve, passing the reserved filling to spoon on top.

NOTE: Store these roulades, covered in waxed paper, in the refrigerator for up to 4 days.

Chocolate Ganache

MAKES: 3 cups
PREPARATION TIME: 5 minutes
COOKING TIME: 2 minutes
CHILL TIME: 30 minutes

1½ cups heavy (whipping) cream
16 ounces (2⅔ cups) semisweet
   chocolate chips
2 tablespoons Kahlúa

COMBINE the cream and chocolate chips in a medium-size glass bowl. Place in the microwave and cook 1 to 2 minutes on high power until melted, stirring once. Stir in the liqueur. Allow to cool.

COVER bowl with plastic wrap and place in the refrigerator to chill or until spreading consistency, 30 minutes.

Honey Bun Cake

SERVES: 20
PREPARATION TIME: 10 minutes
BAKING TIME: 38 to 40 minutes
ASSEMBLY TIME: 3 minutes

Vegetable oil cooking spray, for
   misting the pan
1 package (18.25 ounces) plain yellow
   cake mix
1 cup sour cream
¾ cup vegetable oil, such as canola,
   corn, safflower, soybean, or
   sunflower
4 large eggs
⅓ cup honey
⅓ cup packed light brown sugar
1 tablespoon ground cinnamon
½ cup finely chopped pecans (optional)
Sugar Glaze

PLACE a rack in the center of the oven and preheat the oven to 350°F. Lightly mist a 13- by 9-inch baking pan with vegetable oil cooking spray. Set the pan aside.

PLACE the cake mix, sour cream, oil, and eggs in a large mixing bowl. Blend with an electric mixer on low speed for 1 minute. Stop the machine and scrape down the sides of the bowl with a rubber spatula. Increase the mixer speed to medium and beat 2 minutes more, scraping down the sides again if needed. The

batter should look thick and well blended. Pour the batter into the prepared pan, smoothing it out with the rubber spatula.

DRIZZLE the honey on top of the batter, then sprinkle on the brown sugar, cinnamon, and, if using, pecans. With a dinner knife, swirl through these ingredients to blend them slightly. Place the pan in the oven.

BAKE the cake until it is golden and springs back when lightly pressed with your finger, 38 to 40 minutes. Remove from the oven and place it on a wire rack while you prepare the glaze.

DRIZZLE the glaze over the top of the hot cake in the pan. Allow the cake to cool for 20 minutes more before cutting it into squares and serving warm.

Sugar Glaze

MAKES: about 1 cup
PREPARATION TIME: 4 minutes

2 cups confectioners' sugar, sifted
⅓ cup milk
1 teaspoon pure vanilla extract

PLACE the confectioners' sugar, milk, and vanilla in a small mixing bowl and stir until the mixture is well combined.

NOTE: Store this cake, covered in plastic wrap, at room temperature for up to 1 week. Or freeze it, wrapped in aluminum foil, for up to 6 months.

Family Christmas Brunch

Spend quality time with family on Christmas morning rather than time in the kitchen. You can make these recipes two days to six months ahead and just reheat them briefly before serving.

Garlicky Sausage and Cheese Grits

SERVES: 6 to 8
PREPARATION TIME: 15 minutes
BAKING TIME: 35 to 40 minutes

Vegetable oil cooking spray, for misting the baking dish
4 cups water
1 cup quick (not instant) grits
1 package (8 ounces; 2 cups) pre-shredded sharp Cheddar cheese
6 ounces Velveeta, cut into pieces
3 large cloves garlic, squeezed through a garlic press
4 tablespoons (½ stick) butter, cut into pieces
3 large eggs, lightly beaten
1 teaspoon Worcestershire sauce

PREHEAT the oven to 400°F.
LIGHTLY mist an 11- by 7-inch (2-quart) glass or ceramic baking dish with vegetable oil cooking spray and set it aside. Pour the 4 cups of water into a large saucepan over medium-high heat. When the water comes to a boil, stir in the grits, then cover the pan, reduce the heat to low, and let simmer for 5 minutes, stirring occasionally. Remove the pan from the heat, add the cheeses, the garlic, and the butter and stir until they are melted. Add the eggs and the Worcestershire sauce and stir until well combined. Pour the grits mixture into the prepared baking dish.
BAKE the grits until they are golden brown and bubbling, 35 to 40 minutes. Let them rest for 10 minutes before serving.

NOTE: Make this grits casserole up to 2 days in advance; just reheat in the microwave to serve.

Sour Cream Cinnamon Loaf

MAKES: 1 loaf
PREPARATION TIME: 10 minutes
BAKING TIME: 43 to 45 minutes

Vegetable oil cooking spray, for misting the loaf pan
Flour, for dusting the loaf pan
1 box (17.4 ounces) cinnamon swirl quick bread and coffee cake mix
1 cup reduced-fat sour cream
1 large egg
3 tablespoons water
¼ cup pre-chopped pecans (optional)

PLACE a rack in the center of the oven and preheat the oven to 350°F.
LIGHTLY mist a 8- by 4-inch loaf pan with vegetable oil cooking spray, then dust it with flour. Shake out the excess flour. Set the loaf pan aside.
SET aside the packets of glaze and swirl topping mix from the bread mix. Place the bread mix, sour cream, egg, and the 3 tablespoons of water in a large mixing bowl. Beat with an electric mixer on low speed for 20 seconds. Stop the machine and scrape down the sides of the bowl with a rubber spatula. Increase the mixer speed to medium and beat 1 minute more, scraping down the sides again if needed. The batter should be well combined and thick. Pour half to two-thirds of the batter into the prepared loaf pan.
KNEAD the packet of glaze with your fingers a few times, then open it and squeeze the contents evenly over the batter. Place the pecans, if using, in a small bowl and stir in the swirl topping mix. Sprinkle half of the swirl topping mixture over the batter. With a rubber spatula, spread the remaining batter over the top. Sprinkle the remaining half of the swirl topping mixture over the loaf.

Sour Cream Cinnamon Loaf

BAKE the loaf until it springs back when lightly pressed with a finger, 43 to 45 minutes. Remove the loaf pan from the oven and place it on a wire rack to cool for 10 minutes. Then run a long, sharp knife around the edges of the loaf and serve warm slices right from the pan if desired.

NOTE: Wrap loaf in aluminum foil, place in a zipper-lock bag, and store in the freezer for up to 6 months.

Spiced Cider Mix

MAKES: 3 cups
PREPARATION TIME: 10 minutes

1 cup orange breakfast drink mix
1 cup sugar
½ cup instant tea
1 package (4 ounces) sweetened
   lemonade drink mix
½ teaspoon ground cinnamon
¼ teaspoon ground cloves
¼ teaspoon ground allspice
Red cinnamon candies

STIR together first 7 ingredients in a large bowl. Store in an airtight container. **TO SERVE,** combine 3 tablespoons Spiced Cider Mix, 1 teaspoon cinnamon candies, and 1 cup boiling water. Stir well.

NOTE: Mix can be frozen up to 1 month.

Banana Muffins with Big Blackberries and Sugar Crust

MAKES: 20 muffins
PREPARATION TIME: 12 minutes
BAKING TIME: 21 to 23 minutes

Vegetable oil cooking spray, for
   misting the pans
8 tablespoons (1 stick) unsalted
   butter, at room temperature
1 cup packed light brown sugar
2 large eggs
1 small banana
3 cups self-rising flour
1½ cups buttermilk
¼ teaspoon ground nutmeg
½ cup large fresh blackberries (about
   12), rinsed and drained
1 tablespoon coarse sugar, for
   sprinkling on top

Banana Muffins with
Big Blackberries and Sugar Crust

We love these sugar-sprinkled muffins served warm, split, and dabbed with butter.

PLACE a rack in the center of the oven and preheat the oven to 400°F. Mist the bottom of 20 muffin cups with the vegetable oil cooking spray. Set the pans aside.

PLACE the butter and sugar in a large mixing bowl. Beat with an electric mixer on medium speed until the mixture is creamy and light, 1 to 2 minutes. Add the eggs and beat again until the mixture lightens and is lemon-colored, 30 seconds. Slice the banana into the bowl. Add 1½ cups of the flour, 1 cup of the buttermilk, and the nutmeg. Stir the ingredients with a wooden spoon just until combined, 10 strokes. Add the remaining flour and buttermilk and stir with the spoon to just combine the ingredients, 10 strokes more. The batter will still be a little lumpy. Fold in the blackberries.

SPOON or scoop ⅓ cup of the batter into each prepared muffin cup, filling it three-quarters full. Sprinkle the tops with the coarse sugar and place the pans in the oven.

BAKE the muffins until they are lightly golden and just spring back when they are lightly pressed with your finger, 21 to 23 minutes. Remove the pans from the oven; immediately remove muffins from pans by running a dinner knife around the edges of the muffins, lift them up from the bottom of the pan using the end of the knife, and pick them out of the cups carefully with your fingertips. Serve warm.

NOTE: Store these muffins, in a cake saver or under a glass dome, at room temperature for up to 5 days. Or freeze them, wrapped in aluminum foil or in a cake saver, for up to 6 months; thaw the muffins overnight in the refrigerator before serving.

The Season Is the Reason for Slow Cookers

Whether you're working or shopping all day, your slow cooker lets you come home to a comforting dinner that's ready to serve. You can also depend on a slow cooker to help free up oven space while cooking the big feast.

Chocolate Chip Pudding Cake

SERVES: 12
PREPARATION TIME: 8 minutes
COOKING TIME: on high 3 hours or on low 6 hours

1 package (18.25 ounces) plain devil's food cake mix
1 package (3.9 ounces) milk chocolate or chocolate instant pudding mix
1 container (16 ounces; 2 cups) sour cream
4 large eggs
¾ cup vegetable oil
2 teaspoons pure vanilla extract
1 cup water
1 package (6 ounces; 1 cup) semisweet chocolate chips
Vegetable oil cooking spray, for misting the slow cooker
Ice cream of your choice, for serving

PLACE the cake mix, pudding mix, sour cream, eggs, oil, and vanilla in a large mixing bowl. Add the water. Beat with an electric mixer on low speed until blended, 30 seconds. Stop the machine and scrape down the sides of the bowl. Increase the mixer speed to medium and beat until the ingredients come together and are well blended, 2 minutes more, scraping down the sides of the bowl if needed. Fold in the chocolate chips.
MIST the bottom and sides of a *5-quart slow cooker* with vegetable oil cooking spray. Transfer the batter to the cooker and cover the cooker. Cook the cake until it is quite puffed in the center and begins to pull away from the sides of the cooker, 3 hours on high heat or 6 hours on low heat. Spoon the warm cake into serving bowls. Serve with your favorite ice cream.

Homestyle Chicken and Dressing

SERVES: 8 to 10
PREPARATION TIME: 29 minutes
COOKING TIME: on high 3 to 4 hours or on low 7 hours

1 rotisserie chicken (2½ pounds each), skinned, boned, and shredded (about 4 cups)
6 cups coarsely crumbled corn bread
8 slices (1 ounce each) firm white bread, torn into pieces
2 cans (14 ounces each) chicken broth
2 cans (10¾ ounces each) cream of chicken soup
1 medium-size onion, chopped
3 celery ribs, chopped
4 large eggs, lightly beaten
2 teaspoons ground sage
½ teaspoon black pepper
¼ teaspoon salt
Vegetable oil cooking spray, for misting the slow cooker
8 tablespoons (1 stick) butter, softened

COMBINE first 11 ingredients in a large bowl. Lightly mist the bottom and sides of a *5-quart round slow cooker* with vegetable oil cooking spray. Transfer the mixture to the cooker. Dot evenly with butter. Cover the cooker.
COOK 3 to 4 hours on high heat or 7 hours on low heat or until set. Stir well before serving.

Homestyle Chicken and Dressing

Chili Mole
Cincinnati-Style

Chili Mole Cincinnati-Style

SERVES: 8
PREPARATION TIME: 15 minutes
COOKING TIME: on low 8 to 10 hours

1 pound ground beef round
1 cup finely chopped onion (from
   1 medium-size onion)
3 cloves garlic, sliced
2 cans (14.5 ounces each) Mexican-
   style stewed tomatoes, with their
   liquid
1 can (8 ounces) tomato sauce
2 tablespoons chili powder
1 tablespoon unsweetened cocoa
   powder
½ teaspoon ground cinnamon
¼ teaspoon ground allspice
8 ounces spaghetti, cooked and
   drained

Chopped onion, canned kidney beans,
   and pre-shredded Cheddar cheese,
   for serving

PLACE the beef, onion, and garlic in a
large skillet over medium-high heat.
Cook, stirring with a wooden spoon to
break up the lumps, until the beef
browns all over and the onions and garlic are softened, 4 to 5 minutes. Drain
the beef mixture and place it in a *4½-
to 5-quart slow cooker.* Add the tomatoes with their liquid, tomato sauce,
chili powder, cocoa, cinnamon, and allspice and stir to combine.
COVER the cooker and cook the chili
until it thickens, 8 to 10 hours on low
heat. To serve, spoon the spaghetti into
serving bowls, top it with the chili, followed by some onion, kidney beans,
and Cheddar cheese.

Hearty Lentil and Sausage Stew

SERVES: 6
PREPARATION TIME: 10 minutes
COOKING TIME: on low 8 hours

2 cups dry lentils, picked over and
   rinsed
1 medium-size onion, finely chopped
3 cloves garlic, sliced
1 can (14.5 ounces) diced tomatoes
½ cup chopped pre-peeled baby carrots
4 cups canned low-sodium chicken
   broth or water (1 [32-ounce]
   container)
1 teaspoon ground cumin
1 bay leaf
1 cinnamon stick (about 3 inches)
½ pound reduced-fat smoked pork or
   beef sausage, cut into 2-inch pieces

PLACE the lentils, onion, garlic, tomatoes, carrots, chicken broth, cumin, bay leaf, and cinnamon stick in a *4½- to 6-quart slow cooker*. Stir to combine. Place the sausage pieces on top. Cover the cooker and cook the lentils on low heat until they have absorbed all the liquid and are tender, 8 hours. Check during the last hour of cooking to see if the lentils need more liquid. Add up to 1 cup more broth or water, if they seem too dry. To serve, remove and discard the bay leaf and cinnamon stick and spoon the stew into deep bowls.

All-Day Beef Bourguignon

SERVES: 8
PREPARATION TIME: 15 minutes
COOKING TIME: on high 6 hours or on low 10 hours

2 cups thinly sliced onion (from 1 extra-large onion or 2 medium-size onions)
1 cup thinly sliced pre-peeled baby carrots
4 cloves garlic, sliced
2 pounds pre-cubed lean beef stew meat
Salt and black pepper
¼ cup all-purpose flour
1 package (8 ounces) pre-sliced mushrooms
1 teaspoon dried oregano
2 bay leaves
1 can (14 ounces) low-sodium beef broth
1 cup dry red wine
2 scallions, both white and light green parts, chopped (for ¼ cup), for garnish

PLACE the onion, carrots, and garlic in the bottom of a *4½- to 6-quart slow cooker* and stir to mix.
PAT the beef dry with paper towels and season with salt and pepper. Place the flour in a shallow bowl. Dredge the beef in the flour, shaking off excess. Place the beef on top of the onion mixture, then scatter the mushrooms, oregano, and bay leaves on top. Pour the beef broth and red wine over the beef.
COVER the cooker and cook the beef until it is quite tender and the liquid has cooked down and thickened, 6 hours on high heat or 10 hours on low heat.

TO SERVE, remove and discard the bay leaves. Spoon the stew into bowls and garnish with the chopped scallions.

White Chili

SERVES: 8
PREPARATION TIME: 15 minutes
COOKING TIME: on high 4 to 5 hours or on low 8 to 10 hours

3 cans (15 ounces each) Great Northern beans, drained
2 cups shredded cooked chicken
1 cup chopped red bell pepper (from 1 medium-size bell pepper)
1 cup finely chopped onion (from 1 medium-size onion)
4 cloves garlic, sliced
1 can (4.5 ounces) chopped green chiles, with their liquid
1 tablespoon ground cumin
1 teaspoon dried oregano
½ teaspoon salt
2 cans (14 ounces each) low-sodium chicken broth
2 cups tortilla chips
Lime wedges, fresh cilantro sprigs, and reduced-fat sour cream, for serving

PLACE the beans, chicken, bell pepper, onion, garlic, chiles, cumin, oregano, salt, and broth in a *4½- to 6-quart slow cooker*. Stir to combine.
COVER the cooker and cook the chili until bubbling, the ingredients have cooked down, and the liquid has thickened, 4 to 5 hours on high heat or 8 to 10 hours on low heat. If desired, just before serving, crush the tortilla chips into roughly ½-inch pieces, add them to the chili, and stir until they soften (or garnish the chili with them). Spoon the chili into bowls and serve with lime wedges, cilantro, and sour cream.

Sweet Potato Casserole with Pecan Topping

SERVES: 8
PREPARATION TIME: 14 minutes
COOKING TIME: on high 3 to 4 hours

2 cans (29 ounces each) sweet potatoes in syrup, drained and mashed (about 4 cups mashed)
⅓ cup butter, melted
½ cup granulated sugar
3 tablespoons light brown sugar
2 large eggs, lightly beaten
1 teaspoon pure vanilla extract
½ teaspoon ground cinnamon
¼ teaspoon ground nutmeg
⅓ cup heavy (whipping) cream
Vegetable oil cooking spray, for misting the slow cooker
¾ cup chopped pecans
¾ cup firmly packed light brown sugar
¼ cup all-purpose flour
2 tablespoons (¼ stick) butter, melted

COMBINE first 8 ingredients in a large mixing bowl and beat with an electric mixer on medium speed until smooth. Add whipping cream and stir well. Mist the bottom and sides of a *3-quart slow cooker* with vegetable oil cooking spray. Transfer the sweet potato mixture to the cooker.
COMBINE pecans and remaining 3 ingredients in a small bowl. Sprinkle over sweet potatoes.
COVER the cooker and cook 3 to 4 hours on high heat.

A slow cooker comes in really handy for keeping food warm, if you're taking your dish to a gathering of any kind.

Gingerbread House

Sweet on Gingerbread

The tantalizing aroma of these cakes and cookies will bring back
fond memories and make new ones as well.

Gingerbread House

MAKES: 1 gingerbread house
PREPARATION TIME: 45 minutes
BAKING TIME: 25 minutes
COOLING TIME: Overnight
ASSEMBLY TIME: 1 hour

3 (14.5-ounce) packages gingerbread
    mix
6 tablespoons all-purpose flour
¾ cup molasses
3 large eggs
Vegetable oil cooking spray, for
    misting cookie sheets
Flour, for dusting
Royal Icing
Assorted candies and snacks for
    decoration (see box)

PLACE gingerbread mix, flour, molasses, and eggs in a large mixing bowl. Blend with an electric mixer on medium speed until dry ingredients are moistened. Shape the dough into a ball, Cover the dough and chill at least 1½ hours.

PLACE a rack in the center of the oven and preheat the oven to 350°F. Set aside two cookie sheets that have been misted with vegetable oil cooking spray. (We used two 16- by 13-inch cookie sheets.)

SPRINKLE flour over a clean work surface and roll the dough out to a ¼-inch thickness. Using a ruler and a sharp knife, cut two rectangles for roof pieces (each 8 by 5 inches), two rectangles for sides of house (each 7 by 4 inches), and two rectangles for the ends of the house (each 6 by 5 inches). With floured fingers or with a metal spatula, place one of the 7- by 4-inch rectangles and the two 6- by 5-inch rectangles on a lightly greased cookie sheet. Place the two 8- by 5-inch rectangles and the remaining 7- by 4-inch rectangle on the other lightly greased cookie sheet.

MAKE the peaked roof. Using a ruler and pizza wheel, mark the midpoint of one of the 5-inch ends of a 6- by 5-inch rectangle. From that end, measure and mark 2 inches along both of the 6-inch sides. Place the ruler on the dough going from the midpoint mark to the mark along one 6-inch side to form a corner triangle. Cut away and discard the triangle. Repeat this procedure from the midpoint mark to the mark on the other 6-inch side. Mark and cut the other 6- by 5-inch rectangle of dough the same way.

PLACE the cookie sheets in the oven and bake for 10 minutes. Reduce heat to 300°F and bake 15 minutes more or until the dough is lightly browned and firm. Remove the pans to wire racks to cool for 2 minutes. Slide a spatula underneath the pieces of the house and place them on racks to cool completely.

PREPARE the Royal Icing.

WHEN ready to assemble, fill a pastry tube with the Royal Icing, or use a dinner knife to spread the icing. On a large serving platter, join one peaked piece and the 4-inch side of one 7- by 4-inch side piece with Royal Icing at the inside corner seam, generously piping icing along the seam, inside and outside of the house. (Support the pieces with unopened 8-ounce cans.) Repeat the procedure with the remaining peaked piece and the remaining 7- by 4-inch side piece, then join the four pieces at the two remaining inside corner seams as before. Let this frame dry for 1 hour.

TRIM one 8-inch side of each 8- by 5-inch roof rectangle. Place one 8- by 5-inch roof rectangle at an angle over the house, with trimmed edge at the roof ridgeline, affixing along the edges with icing. Repeat with remaining roof rectangle, piping icing generously along ridgeline. Let house set for 1 hour. During this time you can pipe or spread the icing around the house to create candy landscaping. When sides of house are secure, use icing and candies to create a door at one end. Use additional icing to create landscaping and finish the details on the house. (See box for decoration ideas.) Let the house dry out well, a day or so, before transporting.

NOTE: This gingerbread house keeps at room temperature in a dry room for 2 to 3 weeks.

Royal Icing

1¼ cups water
6 tablespoons plus 2 teaspoons egg
    white powder (such as Just Whites)
10 cups sifted confectioners' sugar

WHISK together the water and egg white powder in a large mixing bowl. Add the confectioners' sugar and blend with an electric mixer on low speed for 1 minute. Stop the machine and scrape down the sides of the bowl with a rubber spatula. Increase the mixer speed to medium and beat 2 minutes more, scraping down the sides of the bowl again if needed. The icing should look smooth and thick.

anne's gingerbread house decorations

USE THESE ASSORTED CANDIES AND SNACKS TO CREATE YOUR OWN HOLIDAY MASTERPIECE.

gumdrops
peppermints
peppermint sticks
licorice
LifeSavers
Necco chocolate coins
red cinnamon candies
square pretzels
pretzel twists
yogurt-covered raisins
flaked coconut
green decorator sugar
confectioners' sugar
sugar ice cream cone
(cotton for smoke)

I like the taste of gingerbread prepared from a box as well as or better than any from-scratch gingerbread I've eaten.

Pumpkin Gingerbread

MAKES: 1 loaf
PREPARATION TIME: 10 minutes
BAKING TIME: 45 to 47 minutes

Vegetable oil cooking spray, for
    misting the loaf pan
Flour, for dusting the loaf pan
1 package (14.5 ounces) gingerbread
    mix
1 cup canned pumpkin puree (about
    half of a 15-ounce can)
2 large eggs
¼ cup warm water
½ cup golden raisins

PLACE a rack in the center of the oven and preheat the oven to 325°F.
LIGHTLY mist a 9- by 5-inch loaf pan with vegetable oil cooking spray, then dust it with flour. Shake out the excess flour. Set the loaf pan aside.
PLACE the gingerbread mix, pumpkin, eggs, and water in a large mixing bowl. Beat with an electric mixer on low speed for 30 seconds. Stop the machine and scrape down the sides of the bowl with a rubber spatula. Increase the mixer speed to medium and beat 1 minute more, scraping down the sides again if needed. The batter should be well combined. Fold in the raisins, making sure they are well incorporated. Pour the batter into the prepared loaf pan.
BAKE the loaf until it springs back when lightly pressed with a finger, 45 to 47 minutes. Remove the loaf pan from the oven and place it on a wire rack to cool for 15 minutes. Run a long, sharp knife around the edges of the gingerbread and remove it from the pan. Place the loaf on its side on the rack to cool completely, 20 minutes more. Slice and serve.

Fresh Pear and Gingerbread Cupcakes

MAKES: 14 to 16 cupcakes
PREPARATION TIME: 15 minutes
BAKING TIME: 18 to 20 minutes

16 paper liners for cupcake pans
    (2½-inch size)
1 package (14.5 ounces) gingerbread
    mix
1 cup water
1 large egg
1 medium-size ripe pear, peeled,
    cored, and finely chopped
1 heaping teaspoon crystallized ginger,
    finely chopped (optional)
Creamy Lemon Frosting or Sweetened
    Whipped Cream

PLACE a rack in the center of the oven and preheat the oven to 350°F. Line 16 cupcake cups with paper liners. Set the pans aside.
PLACE the gingerbread mix, water, egg, pear, and, if using, ginger in a large mixing bowl. Blend with an electric mixer on low speed for 30 seconds. Stop the machine and scrape down the sides of the bowl with a rubber spatula. Increase the mixer speed to medium and beat until smooth and thickened, 2 minutes more, scraping down the sides again if needed. Spoon or scoop ⅓ cup batter into each lined muffin cup, filling it three-quarters full. (You will get 14 to 16 cupcakes; remove the empty liners, if any.) Place the pans in the oven.
BAKE the cupcakes until they spring back when lightly pressed with your finger, 18 to 20 minutes. Remove the pans from the oven and place them on wire racks to cool for 5 minutes. Run a dinner knife around the edges of the cupcake liners, lift the cupcakes up from the bottoms of the cups using the end of the knife, and pick them out of the cups carefully with your fingertips. Place them on a wire rack to cool for 15 minutes before frosting.

MEANWHILE, prepare the Creamy Lemon Frosting or Sweetened Whipped Cream.
PLACE a heaping tablespoonful of frosting on each cupcake and swirl to spread it out with a short metal spatula or a spoon, taking care to cover the tops completely. Place the cupcakes, uncovered, in the refrigerator until the frosting sets, 20 minutes. The cupcakes are now ready to serve.

NOTE: Store the cupcakes, in a cake saver or under a glass dome, in the refrigerator for up to 1 week. Or freeze them, wrapped in aluminum foil or in a cake saver, for up to 6 months; thaw the cupcakes overnight in the refrigerator before serving.

Creamy Lemon Frosting
MAKES: 1½ cups
PREPARATION TIME: 10 minutes

3 tablespoons butter, at room
    temperature
3 ounces cream cheese, at room
    temperature
1½ to 2 cups confectioners' sugar,
    sifted
1 teaspoon grated lemon zest
1 teaspoon fresh lemon juice

PLACE the butter and cream cheese in a large mixing bowl. Blend with an electric mixer on low speed until fluffy, 30 seconds. Stop the machine and add 1½ cups of the confectioners' sugar, the lemon zest, and lemon juice. Blend with the mixer on low speed until the sugar is incorporated, 1 minute. Increase the mixer speed to medium and beat until light and fluffy, 1 minute more, adding up to ½ cup more sugar, a tablespoon at a time, if needed to make a spreadable consistency.

Sweetened Whipped Cream

MAKES: 2 cups
PREPARATION TIME: 5 minutes

1 cup heavy (whipping) cream, chilled
¼ cup confectioners' sugar
½ teaspoon vanilla extract (optional)

PLACE a large clean mixing bowl and electric mixer beaters in the freezer for a few minutes while you assemble the ingredients. Pour the cream into the chilled bowl and beat with the electric mixer on high speed until the cream has thickened, 1½ minutes. Stop the machine and add the sugar and, if using, vanilla. Beat the cream and sugar on high speed until stiff peaks form, 1 to 2 minutes more.

Gingersnaps

MAKES: 4 dozen
PREPARATION TIME: 20 minutes
CHILLING TIME: 1 hour
BAKING TIME: 12 to 15 minutes per batch

¾ cup shortening
½ cup molasses
1 large egg
1 package (14.5 ounces) gingerbread mix
½ cup all-purpose flour
2½ tablespoons sugar

Jolly
Gingerbread Men

PLACE a rack in the center of the oven and preheat the oven to 350°F. Set aside two ungreased cookie sheets.
PLACE the shortening and molasses in a mixing bowl. Blend with an electric mixer on medium speed until creamy; add egg, beating just until blended.
COMBINE the gingerbread mix and flour; gradually add to shortening mixture, beating until blended. Cover the mixture with plastic wrap and place in the refrigerator 1 hour.
SHAPE the dough into 1-inch balls and roll in the sugar. Place 2 inches apart on the ungreased cookie sheets. Place the sheets in the oven. (If your oven cannot accommodate both cookie sheets on the center rack, place one on the top rack and one on the center rack and rotate them halfway through the baking time.) Bake for 12 to 15 minutes. Allow the cookies to cool 2 minutes on the sheets and then transfer to wire racks and allow them to cool completely.

Jolly Gingerbread Men

MAKES: 10 (4-inch) cookies
PREPARATION TIME: 30 minutes
BAKING TIME: 11 minutes per batch
CHILLING TIME: at least 1½ hours

1 package (14.5 ounces) gingerbread mix
2 tablespoons all-purpose flour
¼ cup molasses
1 large egg
Vegetable oil cooking spray, for misting cookie sheets
Flour, for dusting
1 tube (6 ounces) white decorator icing
Red cinnamon candies
Raisins

PLACE the gingerbread mix, flour, molasses, and egg in a large mixing bowl. Blend with an electric mixer on medium speed until dry ingredients are moistened. Shape the dough into a ball. Cover the dough with plastic wrap and place it in the refrigerator to chill at least 1½ hours.
PLACE a rack in the center of the oven and preheat the oven to 350°F. Lightly mist two cookie sheets with vegetable oil cooking spray. Set the pans aside.
REMOVE the dough from the refrigerator. Dust a work surface with flour. Roll the dough to ¼-inch thickness. Cut the dough with 4-inch gingerbread cutters and place them on cookie sheets. Bake the cookies for 10 to 11 minutes. Allow the cookies to cool 2 minutes on the sheets and then transfer to wire racks to cool completely. Decorate, as desired, with icing, candies, and raisins.

Christmas
Cake Cones

Elfin Delights

These kid-pleasing sweets and treats will bring smiles to all good little boys and girls.

Christmas Cake Cones

SERVES: 28
PREPARATION TIME: 22 minutes
BAKING TIME: 20 to 25 minutes
ASSEMBLY TIME: 15 minutes

28 good-quality flat-bottomed ice cream cones
1 package (18.25 ounces) plain devil's food cake mix
1⅓ cups water
½ cup vegetable oil
3 large eggs
½ teaspoon ground cinnamon
Fluffy Chocolate Frosting
1 cup colored decorator sprinkles, for garnish

PLACE a rack in the center of the oven and preheat the oven to 350°F. Wrap a small square of aluminum foil around the base of each ice cream cone; stand the cones in ungreased muffin cups. Set the pans aside.

PLACE the cake mix, water, oil, eggs, and cinnamon in a large mixing bowl. Blend with an electric mixer on low speed for 1 minute. Stop the machine and scrape down the sides of the bowl with a rubber spatula. Increase the mixer speed to medium and beat 2 minutes more, scraping down the sides again if needed. The batter should look well blended. Spoon 3 tablespoons of the batter into each ice cream cone. Place the pans in the oven. (If your oven is not large enough, place two pans on the center rack and place the third pan in the center of the highest rack.)

BAKE until the cakes spring back when lightly pressed with your finger, 20 to 25 minutes. (Be careful not to overbake the pan on the highest oven rack.) Remove the pans from the oven and place them on wire racks to cool completely.

MEANWHILE, prepare the Fluffy Chocolate Frosting.

REMOVE the foil from the base of each cone; frost the tops and decorate with colored sprinkles.

Fluffy Chocolate Frosting

MAKES: 3 cups
PREPARATION TIME: 10 minutes

8 tablespoons (1 stick) butter, at room temperature
⅔ cup unsweetened cocoa powder
3 cups confectioners' sugar, sifted, plus additional if needed
⅓ cup milk, plus additional if needed
2 teaspoons pure vanilla extract
¼ teaspoon salt

PLACE the butter and cocoa in a large mixing bowl. Blend with an electric mixer on low speed until the mixture is soft and well combined, 30 seconds. Stop the machine. Place the confectioners' sugar, ⅓ cup milk, vanilla, and salt in the bowl and beat with the mixer on low speed until the frosting lightens and is fluffy, 2 to 3 minutes. Add more milk if the frosting is too thick or confectioners' sugar, 1 tablespoon at a time, if the frosting is too thin.

NOTE: Store cake cones in a cake saver or under a glass dome in the refrigerator for up to 1 week.

Jelly Doughnut Cupcakes

MAKES: 22 to 24 cupcakes
PREPARATION TIME: 15 minutes
BAKING TIME: 18 to 20 minutes
COOLING TIME: 20 minutes

24 paper liners for cupcake pans (2½-inch size)
1 package (18.25 ounces) plain yellow cake mix
1 package (3.4 ounces) vanilla instant pudding mix
1 cup milk
1 cup vegetable oil
4 large eggs
1 jar (12 ounces) blueberry or strawberry preserves
½ cup confectioners' sugar
24 whole blueberries or 12 strawberries cut in half lengthwise, for garnish

PLACE a rack in the center of the oven and preheat the oven to 350°F. Line 24 cupcake cups with paper liners. Set aside.

PLACE the cake mix, pudding mix, milk, oil, and eggs in a large mixing bowl. Blend with an electric mixer on low speed for 30 seconds. Stop the machine and scrape down the sides of the bowl with a rubber spatula. Increase the mixer speed to medium and beat 1½ to 2 minutes more, scraping down the sides again if needed. Spoon a heaping ¼ cup batter into each lined cupcake cup, filling it two-thirds full. (You will get between 22 and 24 cupcakes; remove the empty liners, if any.) Place the pans side by side in the oven.

BAKE until the cupcakes are golden and spring back when lightly pressed with your finger, 18 to 20 minutes. Remove pans from oven and place on wire racks to cool for 5 minutes. Run a dinner knife around the edges of the cupcake liners, lift the cupcakes up from the bottoms using the end of the knife, and pick them out of the cups carefully with your fingertips. Place them on a wire rack to cool for 15 minutes before filling.

FIT a pastry bag with a metal tip that has a large round hole and spoon about ½ cup preserves into the bag. Insert the whole tip into the top center of the cupcake. Generously squirt 2 to 3 teaspoons preserves into each cupcake. (You may need to wipe the tip clean as you go.) Continue filling the cupcakes, refilling the pastry bag as needed. When done, sift the cupcake tops with confectioners' sugar. Garnish each cupcake with a whole blueberry or strawberry half to cover the pastry tip hole.

NOTE: Store these cupcakes, in a cake saver or under a glass dome, at room temperature for up to 3 days or in the refrigerator for up to 1 week. Or freeze them, wrapped in aluminum foil for up to 6 months; thaw overnight in the refrigerator.

on the center rack and rotate them halfway through the baking time.) **BAKE** the cookies until the edges are light brown, 8 to 12 minutes. Remove the pans from the oven. Let the cookies rest on the cookie sheets for 1 minute. Carefully remove the cookies with a metal spatula to wire racks to cool completely, 30 minutes. Repeat the baking process with the remaining cookie dough and craft sticks.

NOTE: Store the cookies, wrapped in aluminum foil or in an airtight container, at room temperature for up to 1 week. Or freeze them with the sticks in place, wrapped in foil and placed in a plastic freezer bag, for up to 3 months; thaw the cookies overnight on the counter before serving.

Snowman Cupcakes

MAKES: 22 to 24 cupcakes
PREPARATION TIME: 10 minutes
BAKING TIME: 16 to 20 minutes
ASSEMBLY TIME: 30 minutes

24 paper liners for cupcake pans
   (2½-inch size)
1 package (18.25 ounces) plain white
   cake mix
⅓ cup all-purpose flour
1½ cups whole milk
½ cup vegetable oil
3 large eggs
1 teaspoon pure vanilla extract
Buttercream Frosting
2 cups sweetened flaked coconut
Wooden toothpicks
48 large marshmallows
Chocolate candy sprinkles
3 orange gumdrops, cut into 24 slivers,
   or 24 pieces of candy corn
Red rolled fruit snack or ribbon for
   the scarves
72 green gumdrops

PLACE a rack in the center of the oven and preheat the oven to 350°F. Line 24 cupcake cups with white paper liners. Set the pans aside.
PLACE the cake mix, flour, milk, oil, eggs, and vanilla in a large mixing bowl. Blend with an electric mixer on low speed for 30 seconds. Stop the machine and scrape down the sides of the bowl

Cookie Pops

MAKES: 4 dozen
PREPARATION TIME: 20 minutes
BAKING TIME: 8 to 12 minutes per batch

Vegetable oil cooking spray, for
   misting the cookie sheets
1 package (18.25 ounces) plain yellow
   cake mix
1 cup all-purpose flour
8 tablespoons (1 stick) butter,
   melted
¼ cup honey
2 large eggs
1 cup colored candy sprinkles
48 wooden craft sticks

PLACE a rack in the center of the oven and preheat the oven to 375°F. Lightly mist two cookie sheets with vegetable oil cooking spray. Set the pans aside.
PLACE the cake mix, flour, melted butter, honey, and eggs in a large mixing bowl. Blend with an electric mixer on low speed for 1 minute. Stop the machine and scrape down the sides of the bowl with a rubber spatula. Beat on low speed for 1 minute more. The dough will be thick. With lightly floured hands, shape the dough into 1-inch balls. Pour the candy sprinkles into a shallow bowl and roll the balls in them.
PLACE the dough balls 2 inches apart on the prepared cookie sheets. Insert a wooden craft stick halfway into the side of each dough ball. Place the pans in the oven. (If your oven cannot accommodate both pans on the center rack, place one pan on the top rack and one

with a rubber spatula. Increase the mixer speed to medium and beat 2 minutes more, scraping down the sides again if needed. Spoon or scoop ⅓ cup batter into each lined cupcake cup, filling it two-thirds full. (You will get between 22 and 24 cupcakes; remove the empty liners, if any.) Place the pans in the oven.

BAKE the cupcakes until they are lightly golden and spring back when lightly pressed with your finger, 16 to 20 minutes. Remove the pans from the oven and place them on wire racks to cool for 5 minutes. Run a dinner knife around the edges of the cupcake liners, lift the cupcakes up from the bottoms of the cups using the end of the knife, and pick them out of the cups carefully with your fingertips. Place them on a wire rack to cool before frosting.

MEANWHILE, prepare the Buttercream Frosting.

PLACE a heaping tablespoonful of frosting on each cupcake; swirl to spread it out with a short metal spatula or a spoon, taking care to cover the tops completely. Sprinkle the tops of the cupcakes with coconut.

MAKE the snowmen. For each body, moisten a toothpick or wooden skewer with water and poke two holes, one above the other, into a rounded side of each of 24 marshmallows. Leave about ¼-inch space between the holes. Insert chocolate sprinkles into holes to look like buttons.

FOR each head, poke two holes for eyes near the top of a rounded side of each of the remaining marshmallows. Poke one hole, beneath the eyes and centered, for the nose. And finally, poke five holes for the mouth in a smile shape. Insert a sprinkle into each of the eye and mouth holes and an orange gumdrop sliver into the nose hole.

FOR the hat, cut a strip about 2 inches long and ¼-inch wide from the rolled fruit. Use your thumb to mash together two green gumdrops into a flat round shape. Cut a thin slice off the wide end of a whole gumdrop and press it onto the gumdrop round. Wrap the fruit strip as a hatband, damping the ends to secure it. Repeat with the rolled fruit and remaining gumdrops.

FOR the scarf, cut 48 pieces of rolled fruit about 2 inches long and ½-inch wide. Cut a notch out of one end of each strip about ½-inch deep.

TO assemble a snowman, place a marshmallow body in the center of each cupcake, pressing it slightly into the frosting to adhere. Place two scarf strips on top of the marshmallow, with notched ends out; place a marshmallow head on top of the scarf, securing with a toothpick and pressing down to secure all in place. If the snowman feels wobbly, dampen the scarf ends or dab a bit of frosting on them to help secure. Add another dab of frosting on the top of the snowman's head and place his gumdrop hat, securing with a toothpick.

NOTE: Store these cupcakes, in a cake saver or under a glass dome, in the refrigerator for up to 1 week.

Buttercream Frosting

MAKES: 2½ cups
PREPARATION TIME: 5 minutes

8 tablespoons (1 stick) butter, at room temperature
3 cups confectioners' sugar, sifted
3 to 4 tablespoons milk
1 teaspoon pure vanilla extract

PLACE the butter in a large mixing bowl. Blend with an electric mixer on low speed until fluffy, 30 seconds. Stop the machine and add the confectioners' sugar, 3 tablespoons of the milk, and the vanilla. Blend with the mixer on low speed until the sugar is incorporated, 1 minute. Increase the speed to medium and beat until light and fluffy, 1 minute more. Add up to 1 tablespoon more milk if the frosting seems too stiff.

Snowman Cupcakes

Make-Ahead Goodies for Giving

You can get up to a two-month head start with your holiday gift-making with these recipes that wait patiently in your refrigerator, freezer, or pantry.

Pumpkin-German Chocolate Chip Muffins

MAKES: 2 dozen
PREPARATION TIME: 10 minutes
BAKING TIME: 20 to 25 minutes

24 paper liners for muffin pans
    (2½-inch size)
1 package (18.25 ounces) plain
    German chocolate cake mix
1 can (15 ounces; 1¾ cups) pumpkin
2 large eggs
1 teaspoon pure vanilla extract
1 teaspoon ground cinnamon
1 cup semisweet chocolate chips

PLACE a rack in the center of the oven and preheat the oven to 350°F. Line 24 muffin cups with paper liners. Set the pans aside.

PLACE the cake mix, pumpkin, eggs, vanilla, and cinnamon in a large mixing bowl. Blend with an electric mixer on low speed for 1 minute. Stop the machine and scrape down the sides of the bowl with a rubber spatula. Increase the mixer speed to medium and beat 2 minutes more, scraping down the sides again if needed. The batter should look thick and well combined. Fold in the chocolate chips, making sure they are well distributed throughout the batter. Spoon the batter into the lined muffin cups, filling each liner two-thirds full. Place the pans in the oven.

BAKE the muffins until they spring back when lightly pressed with your finger and a toothpick inserted in the center comes out clean, 20 to 25 minutes. Remove the pans from the oven and place them on wire racks to cool for 5 minutes. Run a dinner knife around the edges of the muffin liners, lift the muffins up from the bottom of the pan using the end of the knife, and pick them out of the cups carefully with your fingertips. Place them on a wire rack to cool for 15 minutes before serving.

NOTE: Store the muffins, wrapped in aluminum foil or plastic wrap, or in a cake saver, at room temperature for up to 1 week. Or freeze them, wrapped in foil, for up to 6 months; thaw the muffins overnight on the counter before serving.

Zesty Toasted Oyster Crackers

SERVES: 8 (makes 5½ cups)
PREPARATION TIME: 10 minutes
COOKING TIME: 3 to 4 minutes

¾ cup vegetable oil
1 package (1 ounce) Ranch dressing
    and dip mix
1 teaspoon dried dill
1 teaspoon lemon pepper seasoning
1 package (10 ounces) oyster crackers

PREHEAT the oven to 350°F.

PLACE the oil in a large mixing bowl and stir in the Ranch dressing mix, dill, and lemon pepper. Add the oyster crackers and stir until they are well coated.

TRANSFER the oyster crackers to a rimmed baking sheet and bake them until they are crisp, 3 to 4 minutes. Take care not to overbake the crackers or they will burn. You just want to heat them through. Serve the crackers warm or allow them to cool completely and store, covered, in a tin container in a cool, dry place for up to 1 week.

Beer Cheese Spread

SERVES: 8 (makes 1⅓ cups)
PREPARATION TIME: 5 minutes

1 or 2 cloves garlic, peeled
1 package (8 ounces; 2 cups)
    pre-shredded sharp Cheddar cheese
¼ cup beer of your choice
1 tablespoon Worcestershire sauce
½ teaspoon dry mustard
Dash of cayenne pepper
Soda crackers, for serving

PLACE the garlic in a food processor (the amount depends on the size of the cloves and how garlicky you want the spread to be). Pulse until the garlic is well minced, 5 seconds. Add the Cheddar cheese, beer, Worcestershire sauce, mustard, and cayenne pepper. Process until the mixture comes together, 30 to 40 seconds.

SPOON the cheese spread into a small glass or ceramic serving bowl and serve it with crackers; or pack it into a small crock, cover, and chill until needed. The spread will keep for several weeks in the refrigerator.

I'll never forget that first taste experience of pumpkin plus chocolate— sheer heaven. And a smidgen of cinnamon seals the deal in my Pumpkin-German Chocolate Chip Muffins.

Beer Cheese Spread

Provençal
Olive Bread

Milk Chocolate Pound Cake

SERVES: 16
PREPARATION TIME: 15 minutes
BAKING TIME: 55 to 60 minutes
COOLING TIME: 40 minutes

Vegetable oil cooking spray, for
   misting the pan
Flour, for dusting the pan
4 bars (1.55 ounces each) milk
   chocolate
1 package (18.25 ounces) plain yellow
   cake mix
1 package (3.4 ounces) vanilla instant
   pudding mix
1 cup sour cream
½ cup vegetable oil, such as canola,
   corn, safflower, soybean, or
   sunflower
4 large eggs
1 teaspoon pure vanilla extract
2 teaspoons confectioners' sugar

PLACE a rack in the center of the oven and preheat the oven to 350°F. Lightly mist a 12-cup Bundt pan with vegetable oil spray, then dust with flour. Shake out the excess flour. Set the pan aside.
BREAK up the milk chocolate bars into 1-inch pieces and place them in a food processor fitted with the steel blade. Pulse on and off 12 to 15 times until the candy is grated but not a powder. (Some pieces may be large and some may be small.) Set the processor bowl aside.
PLACE the cake mix, pudding mix, sour cream, oil, eggs, and vanilla in a large mixing bowl. Blend with an electric mixer on low speed for 1 minute. Stop the machine and scrape down the sides of the bowl with a rubber spatula. Increase the mixer speed to medium and beat 2 minutes more, scraping down the sides again if needed. The batter should look thick and smooth. Fold in the grated chocolate until it is well distributed. Pour the batter into the prepared pan, smoothing it out with the rubber spatula. Place the pan in the oven.
BAKE the cake until it is golden brown and springs back when lightly pressed with your finger, 55 to 60 minutes. Remove the pan from the oven and place it on a wire rack to cool for 20 minutes.

Provençal Olive Bread

MAKES: 2 miniature loaves
PREPARATION TIME: 15 minutes
BAKING TIME: 25 to 28 minutes

Vegetable oil cooking spray, for
   misting the loaf pans
1½ cups biscuit mix, such as Bisquick,
   plus more for dusting the pans
2 to 3 slices ham (for ½ cup
   chopped)
½ cup pre-sliced green olives
1 large egg, lightly beaten
4 tablespoons olive oil
⅓ cup dry white wine
½ cup pre-shredded Gruyère or Swiss
   cheese

PLACE a rack in the center of the oven and preheat the oven to 400°F.
LIGHTLY mist two miniature loaf pans (5½- by 3-inches) with vegetable oil cooking spray, then dust them with biscuit mix. Shake out the excess.

PLACE the ham and olives in a food processor and pulse until finely chopped. Place 1½ cups of the biscuit mix and the egg, olive oil, and wine in a large mixing bowl. Fold in the chopped ham and olives and the cheese; stir until the ingredients are just incorporated. Divide the batter evenly among the prepared pans.
BAKE the loaves until they are golden brown and spring back when lightly pressed with a finger, 25 to 28 minutes. Remove the pans from the oven and place them on a wire rack to cool for 5 minutes. Run a long, sharp knife around the edges of the loaves, invert them onto your hand, then invert them again onto the rack so they are right side up. Allow the loaves to cool another 15 minutes

NOTE: Freeze the loves for up to 3 months, well wrapped in aluminum foil and placed in a zipper-lock bag. To serve, thaw in the refrigerator overnight.

Run a long, sharp knife around the edge of the cake and invert it onto the rack to cool completely, 20 minutes more. **PLACE** the cake on a serving platter and sift confectioners' sugar over the top.

NOTE: Store this cake, covered in plastic wrap or aluminum foil, at room temperature for up to 1 week. Or freeze it, wrapped in foil, for up to 6 months; thaw the cake overnight on the counter before serving.

Lemon-Poppy Seed Loaf

MAKES: 1 loaf
PREPARATION TIME: 10 minutes
BAKING TIME: 43 to 47 minutes

Vegetable oil cooking spray, for misting the loaf pan
Flour, for dusting the pan
1 package (15.8 ounces) lemon-poppy seed muffin mix
1 cup lemon yogurt
2 large eggs
¼ cup vegetable oil
1 cup confectioners' sugar
1 tablespoon fresh lemon juice
1 to 3 teaspoons water

PLACE a rack in the center of the oven and preheat the oven to 350°F.
LIGHTLY mist a 9- by 5-inch loaf pan with vegetable oil cooking spray, then dust it with flour. Shake out the excess flour. Set the loaf pan aside.
PLACE the muffin mix, yogurt, eggs, and oil in a large mixing bowl. Beat with an electric mixer on low speed for 20 seconds. Stop the machine and scrape down the sides of the bowl with a rubber spatula. Increase the mixer speed to medium and beat 1 minute more, scraping down the sides again if needed. The batter should be well combined. Scrape the batter into the prepared loaf pan.
BAKE the loaf until it springs back when lightly pressed with a finger, 43 to 47 minutes. Remove the loaf pan from the oven and place it on a wire rack to cool for 15 minutes. Run a long, sharp knife around the edges of the loaf and remove it from the pan. Place the loaf on its side on the rack to cool completely, 20 minutes more.

MEANWHILE, place confectioners' sugar and lemon juice in a small mixing bowl. Add the 1 teaspoon of water and stir to combine. The glaze should be thick but spreadable. If needed, add up to 2 teaspoons more water to the glaze to get the proper consistency. When loaf has cooled, spoon glaze over the top, allowing it to dribble down the sides.

Orange and Cranberry Scones

MAKES: 8 scones
PREPARATION TIME: 12 minutes
BAKING TIME: 20 minutes

3 cups plus 2 tablespoons biscuit mix, such as Bisquick
4 tablespoons (½ stick) cold unsalted butter, cut into pieces, plus more for serving
⅓ cup plus 1 tablespoon sugar
1 heaping teaspoon grated orange zest (from 1 medium-size orange)
⅓ cup dried cranberries, chopped
1 large egg, lightly beaten
½ cup buttermilk
Butter and jam, for serving

PLACE a rack in the center of the oven and preheat the oven to 375°F.
PLACE the 3 cups of biscuit mix and the butter in a large mixing bowl. With a pastry blender or two knives, cut the butter into the biscuit mix until the mixture resembles peas. Stir in ⅓ cup of sugar, the orange zest, and cranberries. Add the egg and buttermilk and stir until the dough is well blended. It should be sticky but not wet.
DUST a clean work surface with 1 tablespoon of the biscuit mix. Turn the dough out on the surface and knead it 6 to 8 times on the floured surface. Sprinkle the remaining 1 tablespoon of biscuit mix over the dough and press dough into a 10-inch round about ⅝-inch thick. Using a sharp knife, cut the dough into eight wedges. Place the wedges on an ungreased baking sheet, slightly apart for a crusty edge or just touching for a softer scone. Sprinkle the tops with the remaining 1 tablespoon of sugar.
BAKE the scones until they are light brown, 20 minutes. Remove the baking sheet from the oven and, using a metal spatula, transfer the scones to a serving plate. Serve with butter and jam.

Orange and Cranberry Scones

Easy Sweet and Hot Pickles

MAKES: 4 to 5 cups
PREPARATION TIME: 30 minutes
MARINATE TIME: 3 days

1 quart whole dill pickles, drained
1 quart whole sour pickles, drained
4 cups sugar
4 cloves garlic, thinly sliced
1 fresh serrano pepper, thinly sliced

CUT off the ends of the pickles and discard them. Cut the pickles into ¼-inch slices. Place a layer of the pickle slices in the bottom of a very large glass, stainless steel, or ceramic bowl (do not use an aluminum one). Sprinkle some of the sugar over them, then scatter some of the slices of garlic and serrano pepper on top. Continue layering until all the ingredients have been used. Cover the bowl with plastic wrap and place in the refrigerator. Let marinate for 3 days, stirring several times each day. The sugar will dissolve as the pickles marinate.

PACK the pickles into four or five sterilized half-pint jars and pour their marinade over them, dividing it equally among the jars. The pickles can be stored in the refrigerator for up to 2 months.

Butterscotch-Pecan Saucepan Blondies

MAKES: 4 dozen
PREPARATION TIME: 10 minutes
BAKING TIME: 30 to 35 minutes
COOLING TIME: 20 minutes

Vegetable oil cooking spray, for misting the baking dish
All-purpose flour, for dusting the baking dish
12 tablespoons (1½ sticks) butter
1⅓ cups firmly packed light brown sugar
⅔ cup granulated sugar
3 cups biscuit mix, such as Bisquick
1 teaspoon pure vanilla extract
3 large eggs
1 cup butterscotch chips
1 cup pre-chopped pecans

PLACE a rack in the center of the oven and preheat the oven to 350°F.
LIGHTLY mist a 13- by 9-inch baking dish with vegetable oil cooking spray, then dust it with flour. Shake out the excess flour. Set the baking dish aside.
PLACE the butter in a 2-quart saucepan over medium heat. Using a wooden spoon, stir the butter until it melts. Add the brown sugar and cook, stirring, until it darkens and dissolves, 3 minutes. Remove the pan from the heat and add the granulated sugar, biscuit mix, vanilla, and eggs, stirring until the eggs are incorporated, 1 minute. Fold in the butterscotch chips and pecans. Scrape the batter into the prepared baking dish.
BAKE the blondies until the center is glossy brown and a little soft but the edges rise up and are crusty, 30 to 35 minutes. Remove the baking dish from the oven and place it on a wire rack to cool for 20 minutes. Cut the blondies into roughly 1½-inch squares.

NOTE: Store these blondies, covered with plastic wrap or aluminum foil, at room temperature for up to 4 days or in the refrigerator for up to 1 week. Or freeze them, in a resealable plastic bag, for up to 6 months; thaw the blondies overnight in the refrigerator before serving.

Lemon-Pecan Biscotti

MAKES: 18 biscotti
PREPARATION TIME: 15 minutes
BAKING TIME: 30 to 35 minutes for first baking, 10 minutes for second
RESTING TIME IN OVEN: 30 to 40 minutes

Parchment paper, for the baking sheet
1 package (18.25 ounces) plain lemon cake mix
8 tablespoons (1 stick) butter, melted
2 large eggs
1 cup all-purpose flour
½ cup chopped pecans

PLACE a rack in the center of the oven and preheat the oven to 350°F. Line a baking sheet with parchment paper and set aside.
PLACE the cake mix, melted butter, eggs, flour, and pecans in a large mixing bowl. Blend with an electric mixer on low speed until well blended, 3 to 4 minutes. Stop the machine and scrape down the sides of the bowl with a rubber spatula. The dough should come together into a ball. Transfer it to the prepared baking sheet. With floured hands, shape the dough into a rectangle about 10 inches long by 4 inches wide

Easy Sweet and Hot Pickles

by ½-inch thick. Mound the dough so it is slightly higher in the center. Place the baking sheet in the oven.

BAKE the biscotti rectangle until it feels firm when lightly pressed with your finger and a toothpick inserted in the center comes out clean, 30 to 35 minutes. Remove the baking sheet from the oven and allow the biscotti to cool 10 minutes. Leave the oven on.

CUTTING on the baking sheet, use a sharp serrated bread knife to slice the rectangle on the diagonal into 1-inch-thick slices. You should get 14 slices. Carefully turn these slices onto their sides, using the slicing knife to arrange them on the same baking sheet. Return the baking sheet to the oven.

BAKE the biscotti 10 minutes. Turn the oven off and let the biscotti remain in the oven until they are crisp, 30 to 40 minutes more. Remove the baking sheet from the oven, transfer the biscotti to a rack, and allow them to cool completely, 2 hours.

NOTE: Store the biscotti in an airtight container at room temperature for up to several weeks.

Chocolate-Cinnamon Biscotti

MAKES: 18 biscotti
PREPARATION TIME: 15 minutes
BAKING TIME: 30 to 35 minutes for first
    baking, 10 minutes for second
RESTING TIME IN OVEN: 30 to 40 minutes

Parchment paper, for the baking sheet
1 package (18.25 ounces) plain
    German chocolate cake mix
8 tablespoons (1 stick) butter,
    melted
2 large eggs
1 cup all-purpose flour
½ cup finely chopped hazelnuts
¼ cup mini semisweet chocolate
    chips
½ teaspoon ground cinnamon

PLACE a rack in the center of the oven and preheat the oven to 350°F. Line a baking sheet with parchment paper and set it aside.

PLACE the cake mix, melted butter, eggs, flour, hazelnuts, chocolate chips, and cinnamon in a large mixing bowl. Blend with an electric mixer on low speed until well blended, 3 to 4 minutes. The dough will be thick and come together into a ball. Transfer it to the prepared baking sheet. With floured hands, shape the dough into a rectangle about 14 inches long by 4 inches wide by ½-inch thick. Mound the dough so it is slightly higher in the center. Place the baking sheet in the oven.

BAKE the rectangle until it feels firm when lightly pressed with your finger and a toothpick inserted in the center comes out clean, 30 to 35 minutes. Remove the baking sheet from the oven and allow the biscotti to cool for 10 minutes. Leave the oven on.

CUTTING on the baking sheet, use a sharp, serrated knife to slice the rectangle on the diagonal into 1-inch-thick slices. Carefully turn these slices onto their sides, using the slicing knife to arrange them on the same baking sheet. Return the baking sheet to the oven.

BAKE the biscotti for 10 minutes. Turn the oven off and let the biscotti remain in the oven until they are crisp, 30 to 40 minutes more. Remove the baking sheet from the oven, transfer the biscotti to a rack, and allow them to cool completely, 2 hours.

NOTE: Store the biscotti in an airtight container at room temperature for up to several weeks.

Chocolate-Cinnamon Biscotti
and Lemon-Pecan Biscotti

Pack biscotti in a pretty glass jar with a lid and attach a ribbon and a couple of tea bags for a gift ready to go.

Casual New Year's Celebration

Ring in the New Year with a simple menu geared around the traditional old Southern "good luck" foods. Let everyone know that a fortune awaits inside each cupcake.

menu

SERVES 8

Black-Eyed Peas, Ham, and Pasta

New Year's Layered Mixed Green Salad

Parmesan-and-Pepper Cornmeal Twists

Fortune Cookie Cupcakes

Black-Eyed Peas, Ham, and Pasta

SERVES: 8
PREPARATION TIME: 15 minutes
COOKING TIME: 12 minutes

Salt, for cooking the pasta (optional)
16 ounces medium-size bow ties or pasta shells
4 cans (14½ ounces each) diced tomatoes with green pepper and onion, drained
2 cans (15.5 to 16 ounces each) black-eyed peas, drained

4 tablespoons olive oil
4 cloves garlic, crushed in a garlic press
¼ teaspoon of cayenne pepper
1 cup pre-crumbled feta cheese
1 cup chopped cooked ham
6 tablespoons chopped fresh parsley

BRING a large pot of water to a boil over high heat. Add salt, if using, and stir in the pasta. Reduce the heat to medium-high and cook the pasta, uncovered, until al dente, 12 minutes.

MEANWHILE, place the tomatoes, black-eyed peas, olive oil, garlic, and cayenne in a large mixing bowl and stir to combine.

DRAIN the pasta well in a colander, shaking it a few times to remove any water that might still cling to the pasta. Transfer the pasta to the mixing bowl and stir to combine well. Serve topped with the feta cheese, ham, and parsley.

New Year's Layered Mixed Green Salad

SERVES: 8
COOKING TIME: 4 minutes
PREPARATION TIME: 15 minutes
CHILL TIME: at least 1 hour

1 package (10 ounces) frozen peas
8 ounces bacon, cut into 1-inch pieces
1 bag (10 ounces) spring mix salad greens
4 hard-cooked eggs, shelled and sliced
4 scallions, both white and light green parts, chopped (for ⅓ cup)
1 can (8 ounces) sliced water chestnuts, drained
1 bottle (15 ounces) Ranch salad dressing
½ cup pre-grated Parmesan cheese
2 tablespoons chopped fresh parsley

REMOVE the peas from the freezer so they begin to thaw.

PLACE the bacon in a large skillet over

Black-Eyed Peas, Ham, and Pasta

medium heat. Cook the bacon until it is crisp on both sides, 3 to 4 minutes, then drain it on paper towels. Crumble the bacon into a small bowl and set aside.

LAYER the greens, egg slices, crumbled bacon, scallions, peas, and water chestnuts in that order in a 4-quart glass serving bowl or trifle dish. Pour the dressing over the salad, then sprinkle the cheese and parsley on top. Cover the bowl with plastic wrap and place it in the refrigerator to chill for at least 1 hour, or preferably overnight.

Parmesan-and-Pepper Cornmeal Twists

MAKES: 1 dozen
PREPARATION TIME: 8 minutes
BAKING TIME: 8 to 10 minutes

1 package (11 ounces) refrigerated
    breadstick dough
2 tablespoons pre-shredded Parmesan
    cheese
½ teaspoon black pepper

PLACE a rack in the center of the oven and preheat the oven to 375°F.

UNROLL the dough and separate it into 12 strips. Holding a strip at one end, twist the other end to form a corkscrew. Place the twists an inch apart on an ungreased baking sheet. Sprinkle them with the Parmesan cheese and pepper, dividing them evenly among the twists. Bake the twists until they are a light golden brown, 8 to 10 minutes. Using a metal spatula, transfer the twists to a serving plate and serve at once.

Fortune Cookie Cupcakes

MAKES: 22 to 24 cupcakes
PREPARATION TIME: 20 minutes
BAKING TIME: 20 to 22 minutes
COOLING TIME: 5 minutes

24 paper liners for cupcake pans
    (2½-inch size)
Parchment paper, for fortunes
1 package (18.25 ounces) plain yellow
    cake mix
1 package (3.4 ounces) vanilla instant
    pudding mix
1¼ cups milk
½ cup vegetable oil

Fortune Cookie Cupcakes

3 large eggs
1 teaspoon almond extract, or
    ½ teaspoon lemon or orange extract
¼ cup confectioners' sugar
White edible glitter (optional)

PLACE a rack in the center of the oven and preheat the oven to 350°F. Line 24 cupcake cups with paper liners. Set the pans aside. Measure a strip of parchment that's 12 inches long and 2 inches wide into ½-inch-long segments. Cut the strip into 24 (2- x ½-inch) pieces. Write the fortunes on one side of each. Fold the fortunes in half, wrap each in a small piece of aluminum foil, and set aside.

PLACE the cake mix, pudding mix, milk, oil, eggs, and almond extract in a large mixing bowl. Blend with an electric mixer on low speed for 30 seconds. Stop the machine and scrape down the sides of the bowl with a rubber spatula. Increase the mixer speed to medium and beat 2 minutes more, scraping down the sides again if needed. Spoon or scoop ⅓ cup batter into each lined cupcake cup, filling it three-quarters full. (You will get between 22 and 24 cupcakes;

remove the empty liners, if any.) Gently press a fortune into the center of each cupcake with a toothpick or a fork, sinking it into the batter so it cannot be seen. Place the pans in the oven.

BAKE the cupcakes until they are golden and spring back when lightly pressed with your finger, 20 to 22 minutes. Remove the pans from the oven and place them on wire racks to cool for 5 minutes. Run a dinner knife around the edges of the cupcake liners, lift the cupcakes up from the bottoms of the cups using the end of the knife, and pick them out of the cups carefully with your fingertips. Place them on a wire rack to cool for 15 minutes before garnishing.

DUST confectioners' sugar over each cupcake and, if using, sprinkle with edible glitter. (Ask guests to break the cupcakes in half and pull out the fortune before biting into cupcakes.)

NOTE: Store cupcakes, in a cake saver or under a glass dome, at room temperature for up to 5 days. Or freeze them, wrapped in aluminum foil or in a cake saver, for up to 6 months; thaw in the refrigerator before serving.

holiday cookbook

Mix and match these easy recipes all season long.

Merry Munchies

Each of these savory appetizers is either make ahead or quick and easy—or both.

Baked Vidalia Onion Dip

SERVES: 12 to 16 (makes 6 cups)
PREPARATION TIME: 12 minutes
COOKING TIME: 22 to 25 minutes

2 medium-size sweet onions, such as
    Vidalias
2 cups (8 ounces) pre-shredded
    Swiss cheese
2 cups mayonnaise, preferably
    Hellmann's
¼ teaspoon cayenne pepper or paprika
Tortilla or corn chips, for serving

PREHEAT the oven to 375°F.
CHOP the onions; you should have about 2 cups.
PLACE the chopped onions, Swiss cheese, and mayonnaise in a large mixing bowl and stir to combine well. Transfer the onion mixture to a 2-quart glass or ceramic casserole or baking dish and sprinkle the top with the cayenne. Bake until the dip is golden brown and bubbling throughout, 22 to 25 minutes.
SERVE the dip warm, right from the casserole, with chips.

The Famous Spinach and Artichoke Dip

SERVES: 12 to 16 (makes 6 cups)
PREPARATION TIME: 15 minutes
BAKING TIME: 12 to 15 minutes

2 microwavable bags (9 ounces each)
    frozen creamed spinach
3 cups (12 ounces) pre-shredded
    mozzarella cheese
1 can (14 ounces) artichoke hearts
    packed in water, drained, and each
    heart cut into 3 pieces
1 teaspoon hot pepper sauce, or
    2 teaspoons chile-garlic sauce, or
    more to taste
Tortilla chips, for serving

PREHEAT the oven to 400°F.
SPEED-THAW the creamed spinach: Place the bags in a medium-size glass bowl and pierce each with a knife. Place the bowl in a microwave oven and cook on high power until the spinach has thawed, about 4 minutes.
SLIT open the bags and pour the spinach into a 3-quart glass or ceramic casserole or oval gratin dish. Add 2 cups of the mozzarella cheese and the artichoke hearts and hot pepper sauce. Stir to combine the ingredients and smooth the top. Taste and add more hot pepper sauce if desired. Sprinkle the remaining 1 cup of mozzarella cheese evenly over the top.
BAKE the dip until it is bubbling throughout and the cheese has melted, 12 to 15 minutes. Serve at once with tortilla chips.

Pecan Cheese Patties

SERVES: 25 to 30 (makes 60 patties)
PREPARATION TIME: 12 minutes
CHILL TIME: 15 minutes
BAKING TIME: 10 to 12 minutes

½ cup pecan halves
8 tablespoons (1 stick) butter, chilled
    and cut into tablespoons
1 package (8 ounces; 2 cups)
    pre-shredded sharp Cheddar
    cheese
1½ cups biscuit mix, such as Bisquick
Dash of cayenne pepper

PREHEAT the oven to 375°F.
PLACE the pecans in a food processor and process them in short pulses until they are finely chopped. Transfer the pecans to a small bowl. Place the butter, Cheddar cheese, biscuit mix, and cayenne in the food processor and pulse until the mixture comes together in a ball. Add the chopped pecans and process until just combined.
SPOON teaspoonfuls of the dough onto two ungreased baking sheets, positioning them about 1 inch apart and making six rows of five patties on each sheet. Or divide the dough in half and shape each half into a log on a long sheet of waxed paper. Bring the waxed paper up around a log and roll it gently on the work surface until the log is uniform and about an inch in diameter. Repeat with the remaining log. Refrigerate the logs for 15 minutes to make slicing easy. Unwrap the logs and cut them into ¼-inch-thick slices. Arrange the slices about 1 inch apart, 30 to a baking sheet.
PLACE the baking sheets in the oven, one on the center rack and one on the upper rack (or use two ovens if you have them), and bake the patties until they are lightly browned, 10 to 12 minutes. Halfway through, move the top baking sheet to the center rack and the center baking sheet to the top rack. Using a metal spatula, transfer the patties to a large wire rack to cool for 15 minutes.

NOTE: The patties can be stored between layers of waxed paper in tightly covered tins for up to 1 week. Baked patties freeze well in plastic freezer bags for up to 6 months. Thaw them overnight in the refrigerator. Let the patties return to room temperature before serving.

Baja Dip

SERVES: 4 to 6 (makes 3 cups)
PREPARATION TIME: 10 to 12 minutes

1 cup (8 ounces) store-bought hummus
1 medium-size avocado, cut into
    ½-inch cubes (for 1 cup cubes)
1 tablespoon fresh lime juice
½ cup store-bought chunky tomato
    salsa
½ cup reduced-fat sour cream
2 tablespoons chopped fresh cilantro
Tortilla chips, for serving

USING a rubber spatula, spread the hummus over the bottom of a 1-quart glass or ceramic bowl. Layer the avocado cubes on top and sprinkle the lime juice over all. Top with the salsa, sour cream, and cilantro.
TO SERVE, place the bowl on a large platter and surround it with tortilla chips. Make sure everyone dips in deep to get all the layers.

Crab Fritters with
Creole Mayonnaise

Crab Fritters with Creole Mayonnaise

SERVES: 8 to 12 (makes 16 to 20
    fritters)
PREPARATION TIME: 10 minutes
COOKING TIME: 6 minutes

¼ cup Creole mustard
¼ cup mayonnaise
2 cups vegetable oil
½ cup biscuit mix, such as Bisquick
¼ cup milk
1 large egg, lightly beaten
¼ cup chopped scallions, both white
    and light green parts
Dash of hot pepper sauce
1 cup lump crabmeat, picked over
Fresh parsley leaves, for garnish

MAKE Creole mayonnaise: Place the
mustard and mayonnaise in a small glass
bowl and stir to combine. Cover and
refrigerate until ready to serve.

POUR the oil into a 10-inch cast-iron
skillet and heat over medium-high heat.

PLACE the biscuit mix, milk, egg, scallions, and hot pepper sauce in a
medium-size mixing bowl and stir
to combine. Fold in the crabmeat.
When the oil is hot, drop in teaspoonfuls of the batter, 8 to 10 at a time. Fry
the fritters until golden brown, 1
minute, then turn them with a slotted
spoon and fry until golden brown on the
other side, 1 to 2 minutes more.
Remove the fritters with the spoon to
paper towels to drain. Repeat with the
remaining batter.

TO SERVE, place the bowl of Creole
mayonnaise in the center of a serving
platter. Surround it with the crab fritters. Garnish with fresh parsley if
desired.

5 fast and fabulous dips

1 **Stir together a full jar of Thai
peanut sauce,** a little bit of pancake
syrup, a dash of hot pepper sauce, and a
squeeze of ketchup. You'll wind up with a
sweet, tangy peanut sauce with a kick!

2 **Mix equal parts mayonnaise and
honey-flavored mustard** to make a
great sauce for dipping chicken nuggets.

3 **Begin again with mayonnaise,**
but this time add a dollop of ketchup,
a spoonful of pickle relish, and a dash of
hot pepper sauce for a speedy rémoulade.
Serve with boiled shrimp or crab cakes.

4 **Start with your favorite bottled
Italian salad dressing** and squeeze
in some fresh lime juice. Add a pinch of
sugar and a handful of chopped fresh
cilantro. It'll be your favorite Mexican dip.

5 **Don't forget the classic:** Combine
a packet of dried onion soup mix and
a carton of sour cream. A chip couldn't
ask for anything better!

5 ways to doctor store-bought cranberry juice

1 **Whip up poinsettia sparklers.** Add a little cranberry juice and Triple Sec to sparkling wine for a lovely red cocktail, perfect for brunch on New Year's Eve.

2 **Make a non-alcoholic cranberry sangría.** Blend cranberry juice and ginger ale. Float sliced oranges, sliced limes, and fresh whole cranberries in the pitcher.

3 **Freeze cranberry juice in ice cube trays** and add to grapefruit, orange, or pineapple juice to serve with holiday brunch.

4 **Or freeze orange juice in ice cube trays** and serve in glasses of cranberry juice blended with a little ginger ale or sparkling water.

5 **Add a dash of creamy piña colada mix** to cranberry juice for an icy pink cocktail. Add coconut rum for extra flavor and fun.

Joe's Zesty Crab Dip

SERVES: 4 to 6 (makes 2 cups)
PREPARATION TIME: 4 minutes
CHILL TIME: 1 hour

1 jar (12 ounces) cocktail sauce
1 tablespoon fresh lemon juice
1 teaspoon Worcestershire sauce
Dash of hot pepper sauce
1 can (4.25 ounces) lump crabmeat, well drained
Tortilla or bagel chips, for serving

PLACE the cocktail sauce, lemon juice, Worcestershire sauce, and hot pepper sauce in a small glass bowl and stir to combine. Fold in the drained crabmeat until just combined. Cover the bowl with plastic wrap and chill for 1 hour before serving. Then place the bowl on a clean tray and surround it with tortilla or bagel chips.

I love homemade pesto, but I also love the time saved by using store-bought in this dandy Blue Cheese, Pesto, and Tomato Stacks appetizer.

Tomato, Basil, and Parmesan Tartlets

SERVES: 24 to 30
PREPARATION TIME: 15 minutes
BAKING TIME: 8 to 10 minutes

4 packages (2.1 ounces each) frozen miniature phyllo shells
12 ounces (1½ packages) reduced-fat cream cheese, at room temperature
1 package (8 ounces; 2 cups) pre-shredded mozzarella cheese
½ cup pre-grated Parmesan cheese
2 large eggs, lightly beaten
1 cup drained chopped oil-packed sun-dried tomatoes, oil reserved
1 cup chopped fresh basil
2 cloves garlic, crushed in a garlic press
Black pepper

PREHEAT the oven to 350°F.
DIVIDE the frozen phyllo shells between two rimmed baking sheets. Set the baking sheets aside.
PLACE the cream cheese, mozzarella, Parmesan, eggs, sun-dried tomatoes, basil, and garlic in the bowl of a large mixer or a large food processor. Blend on the low speed of the mixer or pulse in the food processor until the ingredients come together and are well combined, 1 minute for the mixer and 30 seconds for the processor (stir with a rubber spatula halfway through to redistribute the ingredients). Season the cheese mixture with pepper to taste. Place a teaspoonful of the cheese mixture in each phyllo shell.
BAKE the tartlets until the cheese mixture bubbles and the shells are crisp and golden brown, 8 to 10 minutes. Remove the baking sheets from the oven and serve the tartlets warm.

NOTE: The tartlets can be made earlier in the day and reheated in an oven preheated to 350°F. It will take 3 to 4 minutes.

Blue Cheese, Pesto, and Tomato Stacks

SERVES: 8
PREPARATION TIME: 10 minutes
CHILL TIME: 12 to 24 hours

1 package (8 ounces) reduced-fat cream cheese, at room temperature
1 package (4 ounces) crumbled blue cheese
¼ teaspoon black pepper
½ cup store-bought pesto
¼ cup drained chopped oil-packed sun-dried tomatoes, oil reserved
Fresh basil sprig, for garnish
Crackers, for serving

LINE two 10-ounce custard cups with plastic wrap so that the wrap extends over the edge of the cups. Set the cups aside.
PLACE the cream cheese, blue cheese, and pepper in a food processor and process until the mixture comes together and is well combined, 10 to 15 seconds. Spread a sixth of this mixture in the bottom of each lined cup. Spread 2 tablespoons of the pesto over each cream cheese mixture, then layer on 1 tablespoon of the sun-dried tomatoes. Spread a fourth of the remaining cream cheese mixture on top of each of the cups of tomatoes, then the remaining 2 tablespoons of pesto on each and the remaining 1 tablespoon of tomatoes on each. Top with the remaining cream cheese mixture. Bring the edges of the plastic wrap up over the top of the stacks to cover them. Place the cups in the refrigerator to chill for at least 2 hours, or overnight.
THIRTY minutes before serving, remove the stacks from the refrigerator, peel the plastic wrap off the tops, and turn the stacks out onto a serving plate. Remove the remaining plastic wrap and, if desired, drizzle a little of the oil from the tomatoes over the stacks. Garnish with a fresh basil sprig and serve with crackers.

Blue Cheese,
Pesto, and Tomato Stacks

15 ways to doctor cream cheese for company

BEGINNING WITH AN 8-OUNCE PACKAGE OF CREAM CHEESE (at room temperature), reduced fat or plain, you can make many delicious party-ready recipes:

1 Blend with a can of deviled ham and coarse-grained Dijon mustard to make a little pâté. Serve with little sweet pickles and crackers.

2 Christmas yin and yang. Blend one package with store-bought pesto and another package with pureed, roasted red peppers and minced sun-dried tomatoes. Place the green spread on one side of the dish and the red on the other. Serve with crackers.

3 Blend with a tin of drained smoked oysters and a dash of fresh lemon juice. Garnish with fresh parsley.

4 Blend with a can of chopped green chiles and a small jar of red pimientos. Serve with tortilla chips.

5 Blend with ½ cup (4 ounces) of goat cheese. Add coarse black pepper and serve with toasted French bread rounds.

6 Make herbed cheese by whipping the cream cheese with 1 to 2 tablespoons of cream with 1 minced garlic clove and a smidgen of dried herbs de Provence. Form into balls and coat with paprika, chopped fresh parsley, or chopped pecans.

7 Blend ½ cup of blue cheese with cream cheese and fold in a couple tablespoons of chopped toasted walnuts. Serve with pear preserves or slices of fresh pear.

8 Blend feta cheese with cream cheese and add chopped Kalamata olives.

9 Blend good ol' green pimiento-stuffed olives with cream cheese. Spread onto party rye slices and run under the broiler before serving.

10 Blend shredded Cheddar and deviled ham with cream cheese.

Form into a ball; or pack in a crock and coat with toasted nuts of your choice.

11 Blend with chopped salted cashews and a dash of curry powder. Spoon mango chutney over the spread and serve with crackers.

12 Blend with any smoked fish, such as salmon or trout. Add fresh lemon juice, capers, and minced red onion to taste.

13 Blend with finely chopped and well-drained fresh cucumber. Add a finely chopped jalapeño pepper and a couple tablespoons of chopped fresh cilantro if desired.

14 Blend with finely chopped radishes, green onions, and salt and black pepper to taste.

15 Blend with pepper jelly. Add additional fresh chopped jalapeño pepper if you like it spicy.

Christmas Morning Waffles

Christmas Morning Delights

You won't have a bit of trouble waking the family when the aromas
from any of these breakfast treats waft through the air.

Christmas Morning Waffles

MAKES: 6 to 8 waffles (4 inches each)
PREPARATION TIME: 5 minutes
COOKING TIME: 8 to 10 minutes per batch

Vegetable oil cooking spray, for
    misting the waffle iron
2 cups biscuit mix, such as Bisquick
1½ cups buttermilk
1 large egg
2 tablespoons vegetable oil
Butter and jam or pancake syrup,
    for serving
Crisp bacon, for serving (optional)

PREHEAT an electric waffle iron. Heavily mist the top and bottom of the interior with vegetable oil cooking spray. Preheat the oven to 250°F (to keep the waffles warm until they are all ready to serve).
PLACE the biscuit mix, buttermilk, egg, and oil in a large mixing bowl and stir until the egg is well incorporated. Ladle about 1⅓ cups of the batter onto the hot waffle iron, spreading it out so that it almost but not entirely covers the bottom. Close the lid and cook the waffle for 8 to 10 minutes or until the light comes on to indicate that the waffle is done. The waffle is fully cooked when it does not stick to the top or bottom of the iron and has a golden brown color. Using a fork, transfer the waffle to a heatproof plate and place it in the oven to keep warm. Repeat with the remaining waffle batter.
SERVE the waffles with butter and jam or a pitcher of pancake syrup; include slices of crisp bacon if desired.

Blueberry Streusel Coffee Cake

SERVES: 18
PREPARATION TIME: 20 minutes
BAKING TIME: 45 to 47 minutes

Vegetable oil cooking spray, for
    misting the pan
½ cup chopped pecans
¼ cup packed light brown sugar
3 tablespoons butter, melted
½ teaspoon ground cinnamon
1 package (18.25 ounces) plain yellow
    cake mix
1 package (8 ounces) cream cheese,
    at room temperature
½ cup vegetable oil, such as canola,
    corn, safflower, or sunflower
½ cup granulated sugar
¼ cup milk
3 large eggs
1½ cups fresh, frozen (unthawed), or
    canned (well drained) blueberries

PLACE a rack in the center of the oven and preheat the oven to 350°F. Lightly mist a 13- by 9-inch baking pan with vegetable oil cooking spray. Set aside.
FOR the streusel, place the pecans, brown sugar, melted butter, and cinnamon in a small mixing bowl and stir until well combined. Set the bowl aside.
PLACE the cake mix, cream cheese, oil, granulated sugar, milk, and eggs in a large mixing bowl. Blend with an electric mixer on low speed for 1 minute. Stop the machine and scrape down the sides of the bowl with a rubber spatula. Increase the mixer speed to medium and beat 2 minutes more, scraping down the sides again if needed. The batter should look thick and well blended. Pour the batter into the prepared pan, smoothing it out with the rubber spatula. Scatter the drained blueberries over the top of the batter. Drop the streusel mixture by teaspoonfuls over the blueberries. Place the pan in the oven.
BAKE the cake until it is golden brown and springs back when lightly pressed with your finger, 45 to 47 minutes. Remove the pan from the oven and place it on a wire rack to cool for 10 minutes. Slice the cake into squares and serve warm.

NOTE: Store, covered in plastic wrap or aluminum foil, at room temperature for up to 3 days or in the refrigerator for up to 1 week. Or freeze the cake, wrapped in foil, for up to 6 months; thaw the cake overnight on the counter before serving.

Fresh Cranberry-Orange-Cinnamon Muffins

MAKES: 1 dozen (2½ inches each)
PREPARATION TIME: 10 minutes
BAKING TIME: 20 to 23 minutes

Vegetable oil cooking spray, for
    misting the pan
1 package (15.2 ounces) cinnamon
    streusel muffin mix
1 container (6 ounces; ¾ cup) smooth
    yogurt of your choice (without
    fruit)
1 large egg
2 tablespoons oil or melted butter
1 tablespoon grated fresh orange zest
1 cup fresh cranberries, rinsed and
    patted dry

PLACE a rack in the center of the oven and preheat the oven to 400°F. Mist the bottom of 12 muffin cups with the vegetable oil cooking spray. Set the pan aside.
PLACE the muffin mix and the contents of the streusel package in a large mixing bowl and make a well in the center. Place the yogurt, egg, oil, and orange zest in the well and stir the wet ingredients with a fork to combine and break up the yolk. Stir the wet and dry ingredients together with a wooden spoon, just until combined, 10 strokes. Fold in the cranberries and stir another 10 strokes just to combine. The batter will still be a little lumpy. Spoon or scoop ⅓ cup batter into each prepared muffin cup, filling it three-quarters full. Place the pan in the oven.
BAKE the muffins until they are lightly golden and just spring back when lightly pressed with your finger, 20 to

(continued on page 52)

23 minutes. Remove the pan from the oven and place it on a wire rack to cool for 5 minutes. Run a dinner knife around the edges of the muffins, lift them up from the bottoms of the cups using the end of the knife, and pick them out of the cups carefully with your fingertips. Place them on a wire rack to cool for 15 minutes. The muffins are ready to serve.

NOTE: Store these muffins, in a cake saver or under a glass dome, at room temperature for up to 5 days. Or freeze them, wrapped in aluminum foil or in a cake saver, for up to 6 months; thaw the muffins overnight in the refrigerator before serving.

Little Cinnamon Sweet Rolls

MAKES: 4 dozen
PREPARATION TIME: 15 minutes
BAKING TIME: 18 to 20 minutes

Vegetable oil cooking spray, for misting the cake pans
2 packages (8 ounces each) refrigerated crescent rolls
5 tablespoons butter, at room temperature
⅓ cup packed light brown sugar
1 tablespoon granulated sugar
1 teaspoon ground cinnamon
⅔ cup confectioners' sugar
1 to 2 tablespoons milk

PLACE a rack in the center of the oven and preheat the oven to 375°F.
LIGHTLY mist two 9-inch round cake pans with vegetable oil cooking spray and set them aside.
OPEN the packages of crescent roll dough and divide each log of dough in half at the middle perforated seam. Unroll each of the four pieces of dough. Firmly press together the diagonal perforations within each rectangle to seal them.
PLACE the butter, brown sugar, granulated sugar, and cinnamon in a small mixing bowl and stir to combine. With a small rubber spatula, spread this mixture evenly over the four rectangles of dough, dividing it evenly among them. Starting at one of the long ends, roll up each of the rectangles like a jelly roll. Pinch the long edge of each to seal it. Using a serrated knife, cut each roll into 12 (½-inch) slices. Arrange the sweet rolls, cut sides down, in the prepared pans so that they are nearly touching. Place the pans side by side in the oven.
BAKE the rolls until they are golden brown, 18 to 20 minutes. Remove the baking pans from the oven and place them on a wire rack to cool for 10 to 15 minutes.
MEANWHILE, place the confectioners' sugar in a small bowl and stir in enough milk to make a smooth glaze. Spread or drizzle this over the baked rolls with a dinner knife or small metal spatula. Serve the rolls right from the pans.

Blueberry-Banana Muffins

MAKES: 1 dozen (2½ inches each)
PREPARATION TIME: 10 minutes
BAKING TIME: 20 to 23 minutes

Vegetable oil cooking spray, for misting the pan
1 small ripe banana
1 container (6 ounces; ¾ cup) plain yogurt
1 large egg
½ teaspoon pure vanilla extract
1 package (18.9 ounces) blueberry muffin mix
½ cup finely chopped pecans
¼ cup packed light brown sugar
3 tablespoons all-purpose flour
1 tablespoon butter, at room temperature

PLACE a rack in the center of the oven and preheat the oven to 400°F. Mist the bottom of 12 muffin cups with the vegetable oil cooking spray. Set the pan aside.
PLACE the banana in a small mixing bowl and mash it with a fork; you should have ½ cup mashed banana. Stir in the yogurt, egg, and vanilla just until combined. Set aside.
PLACE the muffin mix in a large mixing bowl and make a well in the center. Pour the yogurt mixture into the well and stir together with a wooden spoon until the wet and dry ingredients are combined, 20 strokes. Pour the blueberries that come with the muffin mix into a strainer, rinse them under cold running water, and drain them well. Fold them into the batter just until combined, another 10 strokes. The batter will still be a little lumpy. Spoon or scoop ⅓ cup batter into each prepared muffin cup, filling it three-quarters full. Set the pan aside.
FOR the pecan topping, place the pecans, brown sugar, and flour in a small bowl and stir together. Add the butter, mashing it with a fork until the mixture is crumbly. With your hands, sprinkle 1 heaping teaspoon of the topping on top of each muffin. Place the pan in the oven.
BAKE the muffins until the pecan topping is deeply golden and the muffins just spring back when lightly pressed

Little Cinnamon Sweet Rolls

with your finger, 20 to 23 minutes. Remove the pan from the oven and place it on a wire rack to cool for 5 minutes. Run a dinner knife around the edges of the muffins, lift them up from the bottom of the cups using the end of the knife, and pick them out of the cups carefully with your fingertips. Place them on a wire rack to cool for 15 minutes. The muffins are ready to serve.

NOTE: Store these muffins, in a cake saver or under a glass dome, at room temperature for up to 5 days. Or freeze them, wrapped in aluminum foil or in a cake saver, for up to 6 months; thaw the muffins overnight in the refrigerator before serving.

Country Sausage, Cheddar, and Apple Bake

SERVES: 8 to 10
PREPARATION TIME: 15 minutes
BAKING TIME: 25 to 28 minutes

Vegetable oil cooking spray, for
    misting the baking dish
1 tablespoon butter, melted
6 slices soft white bread, crusts
    removed
9 sausage patties (12 ounces total)
1 teaspoon dried thyme (optional)
1 medium-size apple, peeled, cored,
    and thinly sliced
1 package (12 ounces; 3 cups)
    pre-shredded sharp Cheddar cheese
6 large eggs
2 cups milk

PREHEAT the oven to 400°F.
MIST a 13- by 9-inch (3-quart) glass or ceramic baking dish with vegetable oil cooking spray.
BRUSH the melted butter on the bread slices and place them side by side in the bottom of a 13- by 9-inch (3-quart) glass or ceramic baking dish. Set aside.
PLACE the sausage patties in a skillet over medium heat and cook until browned and cooked through, 4 to 5 minutes per side. Drain on paper towels. Cut the patties in half and randomly place them on top of the bread. Scatter the thyme and the apple slices on top of the sausage. Sprinkle the Cheddar cheese evenly over the sausage and apples, so

Country Sausage, Cheddar, and Apple Bake

that it completely covers the top of the casserole. Whisk together the eggs and milk in a small bowl. Pour this mixture on top of the cheese.
BAKE the casserole until it puffs up and is deeply golden brown, 25 to 28 minutes. Serve at once.

Sweet Potato Casserole Muffins

MAKES: 12 to 15 muffins (2½ inches
    each)
PREPARATION TIME: 15 minutes
BAKING TIME: 20 to 23 minutes

Vegetable oil cooking spray, for
    misting the pans
1 package (19.1 ounces) cinnamon
    swirl muffin mix
1 can (15 ounces) canned sweet
    potatoes or yams, drained and
    mashed
¾ cup milk
2 tablespoons butter, melted
1 large egg
1 tablespoon grated fresh orange zest
¼ teaspoon ground nutmeg
½ cup chopped pecans

PLACE a rack in the center of the oven and preheat the oven to 400°F. Mist the bottom of 12 to 15 muffin cups with vegetable oil cooking spray. Set the pans aside.
PLACE the muffin mix in a large mixing bowl and make a well in the center. Reserve the cinnamon sugar packet to sprinkle on top of the muffins. Place the

sweet potatoes, the contents of the cinnamon swirl packet, the milk, melted butter, egg, orange zest, and nutmeg in a medium-size mixing bowl and stir with a fork to combine and break up the egg yolk.
POUR the sweet potato mixture into the well of the muffin mix. Stir the wet and dry ingredients together with a wooden spoon until just combined, 20 strokes. The batter will still be a little lumpy. Spoon or scoop about ⅓ cup of the batter into each prepared muffin cup, filling it three-quarters full. Sprinkle the pecans and reserved cinnamon and sugar mixture on top. Place the pans in the oven.
BAKE the muffins until they are lightly golden and just spring back when lightly pressed with your finger, 20 to 23 minutes. Remove the pans from the oven and place them on a wire rack to cool for 5 minutes. Run a dinner knife around the edges of the muffins, lift them up from the bottoms of the cups using the end of the knife, and pick them out of the cups carefully with your fingertips. Place them on a wire rack to cool for 15 minutes. The muffins are ready to serve.

NOTE: Store these muffins, in a cake saver or under a glass dome, at room temperature for up to 2 days or in the refrigerator for up to 5 days. Or freeze them, wrapped in aluminum foil or in a cake saver, for up to 6 months; thaw the muffins overnight in the refrigerator before serving.

Mom's Pot Roast with Vidalia Onion Gravy

Entrées for Every Occasion

Whether you need a main dish for Christmas Day or a busy weeknight, short prep times and handy pantry ingredients make it easy to cook during the time-crunched holidays.

Mom's Pot Roast with Vidalia Onion Gravy

SERVES: 8
PREPARATION TIME: 10 minutes
COOKING TIME: 7 to 9 minutes
BAKING TIME: 3 to 3½ hours

1 boneless beef chuck roast (about 4 pounds)
Salt and black pepper
¼ cup all-purpose flour
2 tablespoons vegetable oil
3 large sweet onions, such as Vidalias, peeled and quartered
3 cups pre-peeled baby carrots (optional)
4 cups halved peeled potatoes (optional)

PLACE a rack in the center of the oven and preheat the oven to 300°F.
PAT the roast dry with paper towels and season it with salt and pepper. Place the flour in a shallow bowl. Dredge the roast in the flour, then shake off the excess.
HEAT the oil in a 5- to 6-quart heavy, covered flameproof casserole or Dutch oven over medium-high heat. Add the roast and brown it on both sides, 3 to 4 minutes per side. Remove the casserole from the heat and transfer the roast to a plate. Place the onion halves, cut sides down, in the bottom of the casserole. Place the roast on top of the onions and cover the casserole.
BAKE beef for 2 hours. Add the carrots and potatoes, if using, to the casserole. Spoon the juices over the vegetables to baste them, replace the casserole lid, and return the casserole to the oven and bake 1 to 1½ hours more or until the beef is quite tender and the juices have thickened.
TO serve, carefully remove the roast from the casserole and slice it. Arrange the slices of beef on plates with the onions and, if using, the carrots and potatoes; spoon the pan juices on top.

BeBe's Cola Ham

SERVES: 12 to 16
PREPARATION TIME: 10 minutes
BAKING TIME: 4½ to 5 hours
RESTING TIME: 15 minutes

1 pre-cooked boneless ham (3 to 3½ pounds), unsliced
½ cup firmly packed brown sugar
1 cup Coca-Cola

PLACE a rack in the center of the oven and preheat the oven to 300°F.
TEAR off two 24-inch-long sheets of aluminum foil. Place one on top of the other, with the shiny sides facing. Starting at one of the long edges, double over the pieces of foil ½ inch, then fold them over again ½ inch to form a seam. Open up the foil and place it, shiny side down, in a 13- by 9-inch (3-quart) glass or ceramic baking dish. Place the ham on top of the foil so that it is in the center of the baking dish. Pat the brown sugar onto the top of the ham, then pour the Coca-Cola over the brown sugar. It is okay if the cola drips onto the foil. Bring the edges of the foil up to meet and double-fold them to seal the foil well on all sides.
BAKE the ham until much of the liquid has cooked out of it, 4½ to 5 hours. Remove the pan from the oven, carefully tear open the foil at the top to let the steam escape, then let the ham rest in the foil for 15 minutes. Transfer the ham to a serving platter or carving board, then slice it and serve.

Fast-Roasted Beef Tenderloin

SERVES: 8 to 10
PREPARATION TIME: 15 minutes
BAKING TIME: 35 minutes
RESTING TIME: 30 minutes

4 tablespoons (½ stick) butter, at room temperature
1 trimmed beef tenderloin (about 5 pounds)
2 teaspoons garlic salt
1 cup sour cream
2 tablespoons prepared horseradish

PLACE a rack in the center of the oven and preheat the oven to 475°F.
MASSAGE the butter into the beef and sprinkle it on all sides with the garlic salt. Place the beef in an aluminum foil-lined shallow roasting pan.
BAKE the beef for 20 minutes, then turn the oven off. Let the beef sit in the turned-off oven for 15 minutes. Remove the pan from the oven, tent it with aluminum foil, and let the beef rest for 30 minutes before carving. The interior will be a perfect medium-rare (about 145°F).
MEANWHILE, place the sour cream and horseradish in a small glass bowl and stir. Slice the beef and serve it with the horseradish cream.

Doctor this pot roast by adding garlic, a bay leaf, or a dash—but only a dash—of red wine.

Pork Fried Rice

Pork Fried Rice

SERVES: 4
PREPARATION TIME: 10 minutes
COOKING TIME: 21 to 24 minutes

3 to 4 (8 to 10 ounces total) thin lean
    boneless pork chops
2 teaspoons olive oil
1 package (6.2 ounces) fried rice-
    flavor Rice-A-Roni
2 cups water
½ cup frozen peas
2 scallions, both white and light green
    parts, thinly sliced (optional)
Soy sauce, for serving (optional)

REMOVE any bones and fat from the pork chops. Slice the meat crosswise into ¼-inch strips; you should have about 1½ cups of pork strips.
PLACE the olive oil in a large skillet and heat it over medium-high heat. Add the pork strips and cook, stirring, until the pork is browned and cooked through, 2 to 3 minutes. Add the Rice-A-Roni and the contents of its seasoning packet and stir. Pour in 2 cups of water and stir to loosen the brown bits from the bottom of the skillet. Let mixture come to a boil, then reduce the heat to medium-low

and cover the skillet. Let simmer for 15 minutes.
STIR in the frozen peas and let the mixture continue to cook until the peas and the rice mixture are cooked through, 3 to 5 minutes more. Serve at once in shallow bowls with the scallions and soy sauce if using.

Christmas Roasted Turkey in a Bag

(pictured on page 44)

SERVES: 20
PREPARATION TIME: 17 minutes
BAKING TIME: 2½ hours
RESTING TIME: 45 minutes

1 tablespoon all-purpose flour
1 turkey-size oven bag
1 (20-pound) whole turkey
1 medium-size onion, halved
1 lemon, halved
1 bunch fresh thyme or parsley
1 teaspoon salt
½ teaspoon black pepper
4 tablespoons (½ stick) butter, melted
2 teaspoons seasoned salt
Fresh kumquats, pears, sage,
    and rosemary sprigs, for
    garnish

PLACE a rack in the center of the oven and preheat the oven to 350°. Dust the inside of a large (14- by 20-inch) oven bag with the flour. Place the oven bag in a large roasting pan with at least 2-inch sides.
REMOVE giblets and neck from the turkey. Rinse the turkey under cold running water and pat dry with paper towels. Place the onion halves, lemon halves, thyme, 1 teaspoon of salt, and the pepper in the cavity of the turkey. Brush outside of the turkey with the melted butter and sprinkle with the seasoned salt. Place the turkey in the oven bag, gather the bag loosely around the turkey, allowing room for heat circulation. Secure the bag with its nylon tie. Cut five ½-inch slits in the top of the bag.
BAKE the turkey for 2½ hours or until the meat thermometer inserted in thigh registers 180°. Let the turkey rest in the bag for 15 minutes, then transfer it to a platter to carve. Let the turkey stand for 30 minutes before carving. Loosely cover the turkey with aluminum foil to keep it warm. Garnish with fresh kumquats, pears, sage, and rosemary sprigs, if using.

Angel Hair with Roasted Red Pepper Sauce

SERVES: 4
PREPARATION TIME: 8 minutes
COOKING TIME: 4 minutes

Salt, for cooking the pasta (optional)
8 ounces angel hair pasta, uncooked
2 tablespoons olive oil
1 cup finely chopped onion (from
    1 medium-size onion)
2 cloves garlic, sliced
1 jar (12 to 13 ounces; about 1½ cups)
    roasted red peppers, drained
½ cup half-and-half
Pinch of cayenne pepper
Basil leaves, or 2 tablespoons store-
    bought pesto, for garnish

BRING a large pot of water to a boil over high heat. Add salt, if using, and stir in the angel hair pasta. Reduce the heat to medium-high and cook the angel hair, uncovered, until al dente, 4 minutes. Drain the angel hair well in a colander, shaking it a few times to remove any water that might still cling to the pasta. Return the angel hair to the pot, toss it with 1 tablespoon of the olive oil, and cover the pot to keep the pasta warm.

who is "al dente" anyway?

I'LL NEVER FORGET SEEING THE WORDS *AL DENTE* IN AN ITALIAN COOKBOOK AND NOT HAVING A CLUE WHAT THEY MEANT. I was raised on soft American elbow macaroni, so if you boiled it to mush it didn't matter because it was going to become macaroni and cheese anyway. But cooking pasta just the right amount of time really does make a difference. Pasta needs to be cooked through yet still have some resistance when you bite into it. And that is what "al dente" means in Italian: to the tooth.

HEAT the remaining 1 tablespoon of olive oil in a large skillet over medium-high heat. Add the onion and garlic, reduce the heat to medium-low, and cook, stirring, until the onion softens, 3 minutes.

PLACE the onion and garlic mixture and the red peppers, half-and-half, and cayenne in a food processor or blender and puree until smooth, 30 seconds. Spoon the sauce over the angel hair and stir to coat it well. Serve at once, garnished with basil leaves.

Spaghetti Casserole

SERVES: 8
PREPARATION TIME: 15 minutes
BAKING TIME: 18 to 20 minutes

1 tablespoon olive oil
1 pound ground beef round
½ cup chopped onion (from 1 small
    onion)
1 clove garlic, peeled and cut into
    slices
1 can (10.75 ounces) cream of
    mushroom soup
1½ cups of your favorite tomato-
    based pasta sauce
1 cup pre-shredded sharp Cheddar
    cheese
4 cups cooked spaghetti (8 ounces
    uncooked)
½ cup water
Vegetable oil cooking spray, for
    misting the baking dish
2 tablespoons pre-shredded Parmesan
    cheese

PREHEAT the oven to 400°F.

PLACE the olive oil in a large skillet over medium-high heat. Crumble in the ground beef and add the onion and garlic. Cook, stirring and breaking up the lumps of meat, until the beef is brown all over and cooked through, 4 to 5 minutes. Remove the skillet from the heat and transfer the beef to a large mixing bowl. (If there is a lot of fat in the pan, drain the mixture in a strainer before transferring it.) Add the mushroom soup, pasta sauce, ½ cup of the Cheddar cheese, the cooked spaghetti, and ½ cup of water and stir to mix. Mist a 13- by 9-inch (3-quart) glass or ceramic baking dish with vegetable oil

cooking spray. Transfer the spaghetti to the baking dish and sprinkle all but 1 tablespoon of the remaining Cheddar and 1 tablespoon of the Parmesan over the top.

BAKE the spaghetti until it bubbles throughout and the cheese has melted, 18 to 20 minutes. Sprinkle on the remaining 1 tablespoon of each cheese and serve at once.

Crabmeat and Sherry Fettuccine Alfredo

SERVES: 4
PREPARATION TIME: 8 minutes
COOKING TIME: 12 minutes

Salt, for cooking the pasta
    (optional)
8 ounces fettuccine, uncooked
1 tablespoon olive oil
1 cup finely chopped red bell pepper
    (from 1 large bell pepper)
1 container (10 ounces) refrigerated
    Alfredo-style pasta sauce
2 tablespoons medium-dry sherry
Cayenne pepper
2 cans (6 ounces each) lump
    crabmeat, drained and picked over
2 tablespoons chopped fresh parsley,
    for garnish
¼ cup pre-shredded Parmesan cheese,
    for garnish

BRING a large pot of water to a boil over high heat. Add salt, if using, and stir in the fettuccine. Reduce the heat to medium-high and cook the fettuccine, uncovered, until al dente, 12 minutes.

MEANWHILE, heat the olive oil in a large skillet over medium-high heat. Add the bell pepper, reduce the heat to medium, and cook, stirring, until the bell pepper softens, 2 minutes. Stir in the pasta sauce and sherry and season with cayenne to taste. Bring the mixture to a boil, stirring. Remove the skillet from the heat and fold in the crabmeat.

DRAIN the fettuccine well in a colander, shaking it a few times to remove any water that might still cling to the pasta. Return the fettuccine to the pot. Spoon the crab sauce over it and stir to coat the pasta well. Serve at once, garnished with the chopped fresh parsley and Parmesan cheese.

Tuscan Chicken, Zucchini, and White Bean Ragoût

SERVES: 4 to 6
PREPARATION TIME: 10 minutes
COOKING TIME: 7 to 8 minutes

2 tablespoons olive oil
½ cup chopped onion
2 cloves garlic, sliced
2 cups shredded roast chicken
2 cups zucchini, cut into 1-inch pieces
   (from 2 medium-size zucchini)
1 can (15 to 16 ounces) white beans,
   drained
½ teaspoon dried thyme, or
   1 tablespoon chopped fresh thyme
1 tablespoon heavy (whipping) cream
   (optional)
Salt and black pepper
½ cup pre-shredded Parmesan cheese

POUR the olive oil into a 2-quart sauce-pan and heat over medium heat. Add the onion and garlic and cook, stirring, until softened but not brown, 2 minutes.
ADD the chicken and the zucchini and continue to cook, stirring, until the zucchini softens, 3 to 4 minutes. Add the beans, thyme, and, if using, cream. Season the ragoût with salt and pepper to taste. Continue cooking until the beans are heated through and the flavors are combined, 2 minutes more.
SPOON the ragoût into serving bowls and serve the Parmesan cheese on the side.

Fast Four-Step Lasagna

SERVES: 8
PREPARATION TIME: 12 minutes
BAKING TIME: 38 to 40 minutes
RESTING TIME: 10 minutes

1 pound ground beef round
1 jar (3 pounds) tomato-based pasta
   sauce
Vegetable oil cooking spray, for
   misting the baking dish
9 no-boil lasagna noodles, uncooked
1 container (15 ounces) ricotta cheese
3 cups pre-shredded Italian cheese
   blend

PLACE a rack in the center of the oven and preheat the oven to 375°F.

CRUMBLE the ground beef into a large skillet over medium-high heat. Cook, stirring and breaking up the beef with a wooden spoon, until it browns all over and is cooked through, 4 to 5 minutes. Stir in the pasta sauce.
MIST a 13- by 9-inch (3-quart) baking dish with vegetable oil cooking spray. Spoon enough of the meat mixture into the bottom of the baking dish to just cover the bottom evenly. Arrange lasagna noodles side by side the long way on top of the meat mixture. Top the noodles with one-third of the ricotta cheese, followed by 1 cup of the Italian cheese blend. Then, starting with half of the remaining meat mixture, repeat the layering two more times. Cover the baking dish with aluminum foil.
BAKE the lasagna until bubbling, about 40 minutes. Remove the baking dish from the oven and let the lasagna rest for 10 minutes, covered, then serve.

which pasta is fasta?

I TIMED COOKING SOME FAVORITE SHAPES AND STRANDS, and here is how long 8 ounces of each pasta took to cook once the water came to a rolling boil.

DRIED PASTA

Angel hair	4 minutes
Penne	6 to 7 minutes
Ziti	6 to 7 minutes
Gemelli	8 minutes
Medium-size shells	8 minutes
Orzo	8 minutes
Rotini	8 minutes
Linguine	9 minutes
Spaghetti	9 minutes
Farfalle (bow ties)	11 minutes
Fettuccine	12 minutes
Dried tortellini	15 minutes

FRESH PASTA

Angel hair	1 minute
Linguine	2 minutes
Fettuccine	3 minutes
Tortellini	5 minutes

Home-Style Macaroni and Cheese

SERVES: 8
PREPARATION TIME: 12 minutes
BAKING TIME: 25 to 30 minutes

Vegetable oil cooking spray, for
   misting the baking dish
Salt, for cooking the macaroni
   (optional)
8 ounces elbow macaroni, uncooked
1 container (10 ounces) refrigerated
   Alfredo-style pasta sauce
1 package (12 ounces; 3 cups)
   pre-shredded sharp Cheddar
   cheese
1 tablespoon olive oil
1 cup coarse bread crumbs

PREHEAT the oven to 375°F.
LIGHTLY mist an 11- by 7-inch (2-quart) glass or ceramic baking dish with vegetable oil cooking spray and set it aside. Bring a large pot of water to a boil over high heat. Add salt, if using, and stir in the macaroni. Reduce the heat to medium-high and cook the macaroni uncovered, until al dente, about 8 minutes. Reserve 1 cup of the pasta cooking water, then drain the macaroni well in a colander, shaking it a few times to remove any water that might still cling to the pasta.
TRANSFER the macaroni to the prepared baking dish. Add the pasta sauce, 2 cups of the cheese, and the reserved pasta cooking water and stir until the ingredients are well combined. Scatter the remaining cheese over the top.
TOSS the olive oil with the bread crumbs in a small bowl, then scatter them on top of the cheese.
BAKE until the macaroni and cheese is bubbly and the bread crumbs are lightly browned, 25 to 30 minutes. Serve at once.

So Easy Tuna Casserole

SERVES: 4
PREPARATION TIME: 15 minutes
BAKING TIME: 20 to 25 minutes

Salt, for cooking the noodles
   (optional)
1½ cups egg noodles, macaroni,
   fusilli, or penne

Sautéed Chicken Paillards with Cranberry-Orange Salsa and Blue Cheese Grits

1 tablespoon olive oil

½ cup chopped onion (from 1 small onion)

1 can (10.75 ounces) cream of mushroom soup

1 cup milk (whole, reduced fat, or skim)

1 tablespoon fresh lemon juice

Black pepper

1 cup frozen peas

1 can (6 ounces) water-packed albacore tuna, drained and flaked

Vegetable oil cooking spray, for misting the baking dish

1 cup potato chips, crushed

PREHEAT the oven to 425°F.

BRING a large pot of water to a boil over high heat. Add salt, if using, and stir in the noodles. Reduce the heat to medium-high and cook the noodles, uncovered, until al dente, 8 minutes.

MEANWHILE, heat the olive oil in a large saucepan over medium heat. Add the onion and cook, stirring, until soft, 2 to 3 minutes. Whisk in the mushroom soup, milk, and lemon juice. Season with pepper, to taste. Stir until the sauce is smooth, thickened slightly, and bubbling, 4 minutes. Remove the pan from the heat.

DRAIN the noodles well in a colander, shaking it a few times to remove any water that might still cling to them. Fold the noodles, frozen peas, and tuna into the mushroom sauce. Mist a 1½- or 2-quart casserole dish with vegetable oil cooking spray. Transfer the tuna mixture to the casserole dish and smooth the top with a rubber spatula. Scatter the crushed potato chips evenly over the top.

BAKE the casserole until it bubbles throughout and the potato chips turn golden brown, 20 to 25 minutes.

Sautéed Chicken Paillards with Cranberry-Orange Salsa and Blue Cheese Grits

SERVES: 4
PREPARATION TIME: 10 minutes
COOKING TIME: 10 to 11 minutes

1 can (16 ounces) whole-berry cranberry sauce

1 can (11 ounces) mandarin oranges, drained

Pinch of ground cinnamon

1 can (14 ounces) low-sodium chicken broth

¼ cup milk

½ cup quick (not instant) grits

½ cup pre-crumbled blue cheese

1 tablespoon butter

Black pepper

4 skinless, boneless chicken breast halves (1 pound), rinsed and patted dry

½ teaspoon seasoned salt or table salt

2 tablespoons vegetable oil

2 tablespoons (¼ stick) butter

2 tablespoons dry white wine

PLACE the cranberry sauce, mandarin oranges, and cinnamon in a food processor or blender and pulse 5 to 6 times to coarsely chop the oranges. Set the salsa aside.

MAKE the blue cheese grits: Pour the chicken broth and milk into a 2-quart saucepan and heat over medium-high heat. When they come to a boil, stir in the grits, reduce the heat to low, and let simmer, stirring occasionally, until the grits thicken, 5 minutes. Remove the pan from the heat and stir in the blue cheese and 1 tablespoon of butter. Season with pepper to taste. Cover the pan and set aside.

MAKE the chicken paillards: Place the chicken breast halves between two sheets of waxed paper on a work surface and pound them to a ⅓-inch thickness with a meat pounder or the bottom of a heavy skillet. Season on both sides with salt.

PLACE the oil and the 2 tablespoons of butter in a large skillet over medium-high heat. When the butter has just melted, add the chicken and cook until lightly browned, 2 minutes. Turn the chicken over and cook the second side for 1 minute. Add the wine, cover the skillet, reduce the heat to medium-low, and let the chicken simmer until cooked through, 2 to 3 minutes more.

TO serve, spoon the grits onto plates. Place a chicken breast next to the grits and garnish it with the salsa.

Thai Spaghetti

SERVES: 4
PREPARATION TIME: 8 minutes
COOKING TIME: 9 minutes

Salt, for cooking the pasta (optional)

8 ounces spaghetti, uncooked

4 ounces (1 cup) fresh snow peas

1 tablespoon vegetable oil

1 package (8 ounces) pre-sliced mushrooms

2 cups pre-shredded carrots

½ pound already peeled and deveined medium-size shrimp

1 jar (8 ounces) Thai peanut sauce

¼ cup fresh cilantro sprigs, for garnish

4 lime wedges

BRING a large pot of water to a boil over high heat. Add salt, if using, and stir in the spaghetti. Reduce the heat to

(continued on page 60)

My children love this recipe for Meaty Ziti and don't even fuss over the spinach!

medium-high and cook the spaghetti, partially covered, until al dente, about 9 minutes.

DURING the last 2 minutes of the spaghetti cooking time, add the snow peas to the pot and cook them until they turn bright green and are crisp-tender.

MEANWHILE, heat the oil in a large skillet over medium-high heat. Add the mushrooms and carrots and cook, stirring, until the mushrooms begin to yield their liquid, 3 minutes. Add the shrimp and cook, stirring, until they turn pink and opaque and are cooked through, 3 minutes more. Add the peanut sauce, stir to mix, then cook until the peanut sauce is just heated through.

DRAIN the spaghetti and snow peas well in a colander, shaking it a few times to remove any water that might still cling to the pasta. Ladle the spaghetti and snow peas into a serving bowl, spoon the sauce over them, and garnish with the cilantro sprigs. Squeeze some lime juice over the top of each serving.

Shrimp Curry in a Hurry

SERVES: 2 to 4
PREPARATION TIME: 10 minutes
COOKING TIME: 6 to 8 minutes

1 can (10.75 ounces) cream of
  mushroom soup
½ cup milk
3 tablespoons sweetened flaked
  coconut
2 tablespoons barbecue sauce
1½ teaspoons curry powder
1 teaspoon hot pepper sauce
½ pound already peeled and deveined
  medium-size shrimp
1 cup frozen peas
1 teaspoon capers, drained (optional)

PLACE the mushroom soup, milk, coconut, barbecue sauce, curry powder, and hot pepper sauce in a 2-quart saucepan over medium heat. Cook, stirring, until

the sauce comes to a boil and is well combined, 2 to 3 minutes. Add the shrimp and frozen peas and continue to cook the curry, stirring, only until the shrimp turn pink and opaque and are cooked through, 4 to 5 minutes more. To serve, spoon the curry onto plates and garnish it with the capers if using.

Easy Beef Stroganoff

SERVES: 4 to 6
PREPARATION TIME: 8 minutes
COOKING TIME: 30 minutes

1 pound beef tenderloin or top sirloin,
  cut into 1-inch cubes
Salt
½ teaspoon paprika
4 tablespoons (½ stick) butter
1 can (14.5 ounces) low-sodium beef
  broth
1 can (8 ounces) tomato sauce
1 package (1.3 ounces) onion soup
  mix
1 package (8 ounces) pre-sliced fresh
  mushrooms
Black pepper
1 pound egg noodles, uncooked
¼ cup chopped fresh parsley
1 tablespoon all-purpose flour
1 cup sour cream

SEASON the beef cubes all over with salt and the paprika. Melt 2 tablespoons of the butter in a 4-quart saucepan over medium-high heat. Add the beef cubes and cook, stirring, until browned on all sides, 2 to 3 minutes. Reduce the heat to medium. Pour ¼ cup of the broth into a measuring cup and set it aside. Add the remaining broth to the beef, along with the tomato sauce, onion soup mix, and mushrooms. Season with pepper to taste. Let the mixture come to a boil, stirring, then reduce the heat to low and let simmer, uncovered, until the stroganoff thickens and the beef is cooked through, 20 to 25 minutes.

MEANWHILE, bring a large pot of water to a boil over high heat. Add salt, if using, and stir in the egg noodles. Reduce the heat to medium and cook the noodles, uncovered, until al dente, 7 to 8 minutes. Drain the noodles well in a colander, shaking it a few times to remove any water that might still cling to them. Toss the noodles with the remaining 2 tablespoons of the butter and the parsley. Cover to keep warm and set aside.

PLACE the flour in the reserved ¼ cup of beef broth and whisk until free of lumps. Pour the broth slowly into the hot beef, stirring constantly. Spoon ½ cup of the hot beef mixture into a small bowl. Add the sour cream and stir until blended. Pour the sour cream mixture into the stroganoff and stir to combine. Raise the heat to medium and cook until the liquid almost boils. Serve the stroganoff spooned over the buttered noodles.

Meaty Ziti

SERVES: 6 to 8
PREPARATION TIME: 15 minutes
BAKING TIME: 30 minutes
RESTING TIME: 10 minutes

1 pound ground beef round
1 can (28 ounces) crushed tomatoes,
  or 1 jar (26 ounces) marinara sauce
1 clove garlic, crushed in a garlic
  press
1 teaspoon dried oregano
1 teaspoon dried basil
8 ounces ziti, uncooked
1 package (9 ounces) frozen creamed
  spinach, thawed
1 package (8 ounces; 2 cups)
  pre-shredded mozzarella cheese

PLACE a rack in the center of the oven and preheat the oven to 375°F.

CRUMBLE the ground beef into a large skillet over medium-high heat. Cook, stirring and breaking up the lumps with a wooden spoon, until the beef browns all over and is cooked through, 4 to 5 minutes. Stir in the tomatoes, garlic, oregano, and basil.

SPOON 1 cup of the meat sauce on the bottom of a 3-quart glass or ceramic casserole. Arrange the uncooked ziti in an even layer on top of the sauce. Pour the remaining meat sauce over the ziti. Spread the creamed spinach evenly over the top with a knife. Cover the baking dish with aluminum foil. (The dish can be made up to 1 day in advance to this point. Refrigerate until baking time.)

BAKE the ziti until bubbling, 30 minutes. Remove the baking dish from the oven, carefully remove the aluminum foil, and set aside. Scatter the mozzarella evenly over the top and re-cover the dish with the foil. Let the ziti rest until the cheese melts, 10 minutes. Serve at once.

Smoked Salmon Ziti

SERVES: 4
PREPARATION TIME: 10 minutes
COOKING TIME: 6 to 7 minutes

Salt, for cooking the pasta
   (optional)
8 ounces ziti, uncooked
1 tablespoon olive oil
½ cup thinly sliced onion
4 ounces smoked salmon, cut into
   slivers
1 tablespoon fresh lemon juice
1 tablespoon capers, drained
¼ cup chopped fresh parsley
¼ cup reduced-fat sour cream
Whole black peppercorns

BRING a large pot of water to a boil over high heat. Add salt, if using, and stir in the ziti. Reduce the heat to medium-high and cook the ziti, uncovered, until al dente, 6 to 7 minutes.

MEANWHILE, place the olive oil in a large skillet over medium-high heat. Add the onion and reduce the heat to medium. Cook, stirring, until the onion begins to soften, 2 minutes. Add the salmon and cook, stirring, for 1 minute. Add the lemon juice, capers, parsley, and sour cream. Cook the sauce, stirring, until it just thickens, 30 seconds. Do not let the sauce come to a boil. Turn off the heat.

DRAIN the ziti well in a colander, shaking it a few times to remove any water that might still cling to the pasta. Spoon the ziti onto serving plates. Top each with a big spoonful of smoked salmon sauce, then grind some black pepper on top.

19 ways to doctor frozen entrées

LASAGNA

With your favorite lasagna—beef, spinach, or chicken—you can have some holiday fun:

1 Sprinkle with additional mozzarella and Parmesan cheeses near the end of baking.

2 Top with chunks of pan-fried Italian sausage and sautéed peppers and onions.

3 Top with additional red pasta sauce of your choice.

4 Top spinach lasagna with sautéed sliced mushrooms.

MACARONI AND CHEESE

5 Transfer to your own casserole dish after it has partially baked and is no longer frozen. Continue to bake. Add Cheddar cheese and run under the broiler just before serving.

6 Add buttery bread crumbs on top during the last minutes of baking to make it taste and look more homemade.

7 Stir in chunks of leftover holiday ham and frozen peas for a quick entrée. Allow the casserole to cook until completely thawed before adding.

8 Stir in sautéed onions and red bell pepper chunks along with cooked Italian sausage. Sprinkle the top with Parmesan cheese and fresh parsley.

9 Layer steamed broccoli florets and half-cooked mac and cheese in a casserole dish. Top with buttery cracker crumbs for a wholesome family holiday side dish.

SPINACH SOUFFLÉ / CREAMED SPINACH

10 Sauté a variety of mushrooms in butter. Serve over the cooked soufflé in a gratin dish or stir into the creamed spinach.

11 Spoon the partially cooked soufflé/creamed spinach into large mushroom caps and bake until the filling sets (soufflé) or bubbles (creamed spinach).

12 Spoon the thawed but uncooked soufflé into hollowed-out tomatoes or red bell pepper boats. First cut them in half lengthwise and remove the seeds. Sprinkle with bread crumbs and bake until set.

13 Layer thawed uncooked spinach soufflé with your basic chicken and rice casserole mix made with mushroom soup. Top with buttered crumbs and Parmesan cheese before baking.

CHICKEN POTPIE

14 Brush the crust of a frozen potpie with an egg yolk beaten with a little water. This helps browning and adds a rustic and homemade look. Sprinkle with the grated cheese of your choice near the end of baking if desired.

SCALLOPED POTATOES

15 For twice-baked scalloped potatoes, stir in sour cream and crumbled bacon. Top with Cheddar cheese. Bake and serve with minced chives or sliced green onions.

BAKED APPLE SLICES

16 Add curry powder and cut dried fruits—such as cherries, cranberries, apricots, pears, and prunes—for a compote to complement a brunch or lunch buffet.

17 Stir together cooked scalloped apples and whole-berry cranberry sauce. Dollop over cooked butternut or acorn squash.

18 Serve the baked apples blended with drained canned sweet potatoes. Bake in a casserole topped with buttered bread crumbs and chopped pecans.

FROZEN CHEESE PIZZA

19 The pizza can be an appetizer for a holiday cocktail buffet when sliced into bite-size pieces. Before baking, top with:
- Crumbled feta, Kalamata olives, and baby spinach
- Roasted red pepper strips and fresh arugula (Add arugula after baking.)
- Fresh tomato slices and fresh basil
- Thinly sliced deli meats, such as prosciutto or salami
- Artichoke hearts, sautéed golden brown onions, and Parmesan cheese
- A drizzle of olive oil; fresh herbs, such as thyme, oregano, and parsley; olive slices; and freshly grated Parmesan cheese.

Love Those Leftovers

Doctor up leftover turkey and ham to make simple suppers after the feast.

Turkey Hash in a Flash

SERVES: 6 to 8
PREPARATION TIME: 10 minutes
COOKING TIME: 15 to 18 minutes

2 tablespoons (¼ stick) butter
Half of a 28-ounce bag of frozen diced potatoes with onions and bell peppers, such as Ore-Ida Potatoes O'Brien
2 cups finely chopped roast turkey
1½ cups low-sodium chicken broth (from one 14- to 14.5-ounce can)
1 clove garlic, crushed in a garlic press
Salt
Cayenne pepper or hot pepper sauce

MELT the butter in a large skillet over medium heat. Add frozen potatoes and cook, stirring, until the onions brown slightly, 2 to 3 minutes. Stir in the turkey, chicken broth, and garlic. Season with salt and cayenne to taste. Let the hash simmer, stirring occasionally, until all of the liquid is absorbed, 10 to 15 minutes.
TASTE the hash and add more salt and cayenne as needed. Serve at once.

Curried Turkey and Artichoke Casserole

SERVES: 8
PREPARATION TIME: 15 minutes
BAKING TIME: 32 to 35 minutes

4 cups shredded cooked turkey
1 can (14 ounces) artichoke hearts, drained and quartered
1 can (8 ounces) sliced water chestnuts, drained
1 can (7 ounces) mushroom pieces, drained
1 can (10.75 ounces) cream of chicken soup
1 cup sour cream
½ cup mayonnaise
1 teaspoon curry powder
Vegetable oil cooking spray, for misting the baking dish
¼ cup pre-chopped pecans

PREHEAT the oven to 400°F.
PLACE the turkey, artichoke hearts, water chestnuts, mushrooms, chicken soup, sour cream, mayonnaise, and curry powder in a large mixing bowl and stir until well blended. Mist a 13- by 9-inch (3-quart) glass or ceramic baking dish with vegetable cooking oil spray. Transfer the mixture to the baking dish and scatter the nuts over the top.
BAKE the casserole until it is bubbling throughout and the nuts are toasted, 32 to 35 minutes. Remove the casserole from the oven and serve at once.

Susan's Turkey Potpie

SERVES: 6
PREPARATION TIME: 15 to 20 minutes
BAKING TIME: 27 to 33 minutes
RESTING TIME: 10 minutes

1 package (12 ounces) frozen deep-dish pie crusts (2 crusts), or 1 package (15 ounces) refrigerated pastry rounds (2 rounds)
2 tablespoons (¼ stick) butter
1½ cups cooked vegetables of your choice
2 cups (packed) shredded cooked turkey
3 tablespoons all-purpose flour
Salt and black pepper
2 cups low-sodium chicken broth

PLACE a rack in the center of the oven and preheat the oven to 450°F.
REMOVE the packaging from the frozen crusts or pastry rounds and set one crust aside. Place a crust or refrigerated pastry round in a 9-inch pie pan that is 2 inches deep. If using pastry rounds, press one into the pie pan and crimp the edge with a fork. Prick the bottom of the crust a few times with a fork. Bake the crust until it is well browned, 7 to 8 minutes. Remove the pie pan from the oven and set it aside. Reduce the oven temperature to 350°F.
WHILE the pie crust bakes, melt the butter in a large skillet over medium

heat. Add the vegetables and cook, stirring, for 1 minute. Add the turkey and cook, stirring for 1 minute more. Sprinkle the flour over the vegetables and turkey, then season with salt and pepper to taste. Cook, stirring, until the flour is incorporated, 1 minute more. Add the broth to the skillet, increase the heat to medium-high, and cook, stirring constantly, until the mixture thickens slightly, 1 to 2 minutes.
POUR the turkey mixture into the baked pie crust. Cover the top with the remaining pie crust. (If you are using a frozen deep-dish crust, it will have thawed by now and will be easy to lay over the top of your pie.) Turn the edge of the top crust under the crimped edge of the bottom crust with your fingertips. Press around the edge with a fork to seal the two crusts together. Make several vents in the top crust with a sharp knife.
BAKE the pie on top of a baking sheet until the crust is golden brown and the juices are bubbling, 20 to 25 minutes. Remove the pie from the oven, let it rest for 10 minutes, then slice it and serve.

Turkey Tetrazzini

SERVES: 6 to 8
PREPARATION TIME: 20 minutes
BAKING TIME: 25 to 30 minutes

Salt, for cooking the pasta (optional)
8 ounces uncooked vermicelli, broken into thirds
1 container (10 ounces) refrigerated Alfredo-style pasta sauce
1 can (10.75 ounces) cream of mushroom soup
3 cups shredded or chopped cooked turkey
1 cup pre-shredded Parmesan cheese
¼ cup drained pre-sliced pimiento-stuffed green olives
2 tablespoons golden or dry sherry
Vegetable oil cooking spray, for misting the baking dish
¼ cup pre-chopped pecans

Asian Turkey Salad

PREHEAT the oven to 375°F.

BRING a medium-size pot of water to a boil over high heat. Add salt, if using, and stir in the vermicelli. Reduce the heat to medium-high and cook the vermicelli, uncovered, until al dente, 5 to 7 minutes, stirring once or twice. Reserve ½ cup of the pasta cooking water, then drain the vermicelli well in a colander, shaking it a few times to remove any water that might still cling to the pasta.

TRANSFER the pasta to a large mixing bowl. Add the Alfredo sauce, mushroom soup, reserved cooking water, turkey, Parmesan cheese, olives, and sherry and stir until well combined. Mist a 13- by 9-inch (3-quart) glass or ceramic baking dish with vegetable oil cooking spray. Scoop the mixture into the baking dish. Scatter the pecans over the top.

BAKE the casserole until it is bubbling throughout, 25 to 30 minutes. Remove the casserole from the oven; serve at once or cover it with aluminum foil to keep it warm. Serve within 30 minutes.

Asian Turkey Salad

SERVES: 4 to 6 as a main course
PREPARATION TIME: 15 minutes
BAKING TIME: 6 to 7 minutes

1 package (3 ounces) Oriental-flavor ramen noodle soup mix
½ cup pre-sliced almonds
¾ cup bottled red wine vinaigrette
1 package (16 ounces) coleslaw mix or broccoli slaw mix
2 cups shredded cooked turkey
½ cup fresh cilantro leaves
2 scallions, both white and light green parts, chopped (for ¼ cup)

PREHEAT the oven to 350°F.

BREAK up the ramen noodles with your hands and place them and the almonds on a rimmed baking sheet. Bake until the noodles and almonds turn light brown, 6 to 7 minutes.

MEANWHILE, pour the red wine vinaigrette into a measuring cup and stir in the packet of seasoning from the ramen noodle soup mix. Set the salad dressing aside.

PLACE the slaw mix, turkey, cilantro leaves, and scallions in a large serving bowl. Toss to combine the ingredients well.

JUST before serving, pour the salad dressing over the salad and toss to coat. Scatter the toasted almonds and noodles on top and serve.

Creamy Ham Casserole

Creamy Ham Casserole

SERVES: 4
PREPARATION TIME: 20 minutes
BAKING TIME: 30 minutes

Salt, for cooking the noodles
  (optional)
4 ounces medium egg noodles,
  uncooked
1 tablespoon vegetable oil
2 cups chopped cooked ham
1 medium-size green bell pepper,
  seeded and chopped
¼ cup chopped onion
¼ cup sliced celery
1 can (10¾ ounces) cream of
  mushroom soup
1 carton (8 ounces) sour cream
Vegetable oil cooking spray, for
  misting the baking dish
½ cup (2 ounces) shredded Cheddar
  cheese

PREHEAT the oven to 350°.
BRING a pot of water to a boil over high heat. Add salt, if using, and stir in the noodles. Cook noodles according to the package directions. Drain the noodles well in a colander, shaking it a few times to remove any water that might still cling to the noodles.
HEAT the vegetable oil in a large skillet over medium-high heat. Add the ham, bell pepper, onion, and celery; cook 5 minutes, stirring often. Remove the skillet from the heat and stir in the mushroom soup, sour cream, and cooked noodles. Mist a 1½-quart glass or ceramic baking dish with vegetable oil cooking spray. Spoon the mixture into the dish.
COVER the casserole with aluminum foil and bake for 25 minutes. Uncover the casserole, sprinkle the cheese on top, and bake until it melts, 5 minutes. Remove the casserole from the oven and allow it to cool for 10 minutes before serving.

Caribbean Turkey Chili

SERVES: 6 as a main course
PREPARATION TIME: 8 to 10 minutes
COOKING TIME: 18 minutes

1 medium-size sweet onion
1 tablespoon olive oil
2 cups cubed, cooked turkey
1 teaspoon jerk seasoning
2 cans (15.5 ounces each) white
  beans, with their liquid
1 chicken-flavored bouillon cube
Hot pepper sauce to taste
1 tablespoon heavy (whipping) cream
  (optional)

Chopped fresh chives, chopped and
  whole fresh cilantro leaves, and/or
  diced mango and red bell pepper,
  for garnish

CUT the onion in half lengthwise, then cut each half crosswise into thin half-moon slices; you'll need 1 cup.
PLACE the olive oil in a 4-quart saucepan over medium heat. Add the sliced onion and cook, stirring with a wooden spoon until soft, 3 minutes. Add the turkey and jerk seasoning and cook, stirring, until the turkey is coated with the seasoning, 1 minute more. Remove the pan from the heat and stir in the beans with their liquid, the bouillon cube, and hot pepper sauce. Fill one of the bean cans with water, add this to the pan, and stir. Place the pan over high heat until the liquid comes to a boil and the bouillon cube dissolves. Reduce the heat to low, cover the pan, and let the chili simmer for 10 minutes.
ADD the cream to the chili, if using; stir, cover, and cook for 2 minutes more. Ladle the chili into serving bowls and serve garnished with chopped chives, cilantro, and/or diced mango and red bell pepper if desired.

Mushroom and Ham Linguini

SERVES: 4
PREPARATION TIME: 12 minutes
COOKING TIME: 9 minutes

Salt, for cooking the linguine (optional)
8 ounces linguine, uncooked
2 tablespoons olive oil
½ cup finely chopped onion
1 package (8 ounces) pre-sliced
  mushrooms
1 cup diced ham or thin strips of
  sliced smoked ham
2 tablespoons all-purpose flour
1 cup heavy (whipping) cream
1 tablespoon fresh thyme leaves, or
  1 teaspoon dried thyme
1 cup pre-shredded Parmesan cheese

BRING a large pot of water to a boil over high heat. Add salt, if using, and stir in the linguine. Reduce the heat to medium-high and cook the linguine, uncovered, until al dente, 9 minutes.

MEANWHILE, heat the olive oil in a large skillet over medium-high heat. Add the onion and reduce the heat to medium. Cook, stirring, until the onion is soft, 3 minutes. Add the mushrooms and ham and cook, stirring constantly, until the mushrooms begin to yield their liquid, 3 minutes. Sprinkle the flour over the ham and mushrooms and stir to coat well. Pour in the cream and stir until thickened, 2 minutes. Spoon in some water from the cooking pasta if needed to thin the sauce a bit. Add the thyme and stir in the Parmesan cheese. Remove the skillet from the heat and cover it to keep the sauce warm.

DRAIN the linguine well in a colander, shaking it a few times to remove any water that might still cling to the pasta. Return the linguine to the pot. Spoon the mushroom and ham sauce over it and stir to coat the pasta well. Serve at once.

Barbecue Quesadillas

SERVES: 4 as a main course, 8 as an
    appetizer
PREPARATION TIME: 15 minutes
COOKING TIME: 8 minutes

1 package (16 ounces) coleslaw mix
    or broccoli slaw
½ cup mayonnaise
¼ cup sweet pickle juice
¼ cup bottled Italian salad dressing or
    sesame salad dressing
1 tablespoon sugar, or more to taste
1 cup sour cream
½ cup fresh cilantro leaves
1 tablespoon fresh lime juice
1 tablespoon vegetable oil
2 cups shredded cooked turkey mixed
    with ½ cup store-bought barbecue
    sauce or 1 package (18 ounces
    frozen or 16 ounces fresh) shred-
    ded pork or beef barbecue, thawed
    if frozen
1 package (8 ounces; 2 cups)
    pre-shredded Cheddar or Monterey
    Jack cheese or Mexican blend
16 flour tortillas (10 inches each)
Fresh cilantro sprigs, for garnish

PLACE the coleslaw mix, mayonnaise, pickle juice, salad dressing, and sugar in a medium-size bowl and stir to combine. Taste for sweetness, adding more

sugar if needed. Cover the bowl with plastic wrap and place the slaw in the refrigerator to chill. It will keep for up to 2 days.

PLACE the sour cream, cilantro leaves, and lime juice in a food processor or blender and puree until smooth, 30 seconds. Set the cilantro cream aside.

PLACE a rack in the center of the oven and preheat the oven to 300°F.

HEAT a griddle or large, heavy skillet over medium-high heat. Brush the griddle or skillet with the oil. Scatter an eighth of the barbecue, ¼ cup of the slaw, and about ¼ cup of the cheese evenly over each of eight tortillas and top with the remaining tortillas. Place four quesadillas on the griddle or cook them one at a time in the skillet. Cook on one side until crisp, 2 minutes. Carefully turn the quesadillas over and cook on the other side until cooked through and crisp, 2 minutes more. Place the quesadillas on a baking sheet in the oven to keep warm until serving. Repeat the cooking process until all the quesadillas are cooked. Slice the hot quesadillas into wedges and serve with the cilantro cream drizzled over them or on the side. Garnish with cilantro sprigs if desired.

Ham and Cheddar Not-So-Impossible Pie

SERVES: 6
PREPARATION TIME: 15 minutes
BAKING TIME: 20 to 25 minutes

Vegetable oil cooking spray, for
    misting the pan
1½ cups chopped ham
1 cup pre-shredded sharp Cheddar
    cheese
½ cup biscuit mix, such as
    Bisquick
1 cup milk
2 large eggs

PREHEAT the oven to 400°F.

MIST a 9-inch glass pie pan with vegetable oil cooking spray. Sprinkle the ham and the Cheddar cheese over the bottom of the pie pan.

WHISK together the biscuit mix, milk, and eggs in a small bowl, then pour this evenly over the ham and cheese.

BAKE the pie until it is golden brown and firm to the touch, 20 to 25 minutes. Remove the pie from the oven and allow it to cool for 5 minutes, then cut it into wedges and serve.

Barbecue Quesadillas

Holiday Sideboard

These festive sides will become the stars of your holiday menu.

Cherry Tomato and Basil Tart

SERVES: 6 to 8
PREPARATION TIME: 15 minutes
BAKING TIME: 26 to 28 minutes

1 package (8 ounces) refrigerated
   crescent rolls
1 cup cherry or grape tomatoes,
   halved
½ cup finely sliced fresh basil or
   parsley
1 cup pre-shredded mozzarella cheese
2 large eggs
½ cup heavy (whipping) cream or
   whole milk
Coarse salt

PLACE a rack in the center of the oven
and preheat the oven to 375°F.
OPEN the package of crescent roll dough
and separate it into eight triangles.

Arrange the triangles in a 9-inch tart
pan or pie pan with the long points
toward the center so that the bottom
and side of the pan are covered with
dough. Press the edges of the dough triangles together firmly to seal them.
Bake the crust until it is lightly
browned and puffed, 8 minutes.
REMOVE the tart pan from the oven and
leave the oven on. Press down on the
crust with the back of a spoon to flatten
it. Arrange the tomatoes, cut sides up,
on the bottom of the crust, completely
covering it. Scatter the basil evenly
over the top, then sprinkle with mozzarella cheese. Crack the eggs into a
small bowl, add the cream and salt, and
whisk to combine. Pour the egg mixture
over the tomatoes.
BAKE the tart until the custard has set
and the crust is a deep golden brown,
18 to 20 minutes, shielding edges with
aluminum foil if needed. Remove the

tart from the oven and place it on a wire
rack to cool for 5 minutes, then slice.

Mother's Party Peas and Artichokes

SERVES: 8
PREPARATION TIME: 5 minutes
COOKING TIME: 4 to 5 minutes

2 packages (10 ounces each) frozen
   peas
1 can (14 ounces) artichoke hearts
   packed in water, drained and
   quartered
½ cup chopped onion
1 cup water
2 tablespoons (¼ stick) butter
2 tablespoons chopped fresh parsley
Salt and black pepper

PLACE the peas, artichoke hearts, and
onion in a 2-quart saucepan and add
1 cup of water. Cover and bring to a boil
over medium-high heat. Reduce the heat
to low and let simmer, stirring once,
until the peas and onion have softened,
4 to 5 minutes. Drain, then stir in the
butter and parsley and season with salt
and pepper to taste. Serve at once.

Creamy Scalloped Potatoes

SERVES: 8 to 10
PREPARATION TIME: 15 minutes
BAKING TIME: 30 to 35 minutes

Vegetable oil cooking spray, for
   misting the baking dish
1 package (32 ounces) frozen hash
   brown potatoes, slightly thawed
½ cup pre-shredded Parmesan cheese
2 to 3 cloves garlic, sliced
Salt and black pepper
2 cups heavy (whipping) cream

PLACE a rack in the center of the oven
and preheat the oven to 400°F.
MIST a 13- by 9-inch (3-quart) glass or
ceramic baking dish with vegetable oil
cooking spray.

Cherry Tomato
and Basil Tart

PLACE half of the hash browns in an even layer in a 13- by 9-inch (3-quart) glass or ceramic baking dish. Break the hash browns apart with your hands if they are still mostly frozen. Sprinkle the cheese and garlic over the top. Season with salt and pepper. Place the remaining hash browns in an even layer on top of the cheese. Pour the cream over the potatoes, then cover with aluminum foil.

BAKE the potatoes until the cream bubbles and the potatoes are tender, 30 to 35 minutes. Remove the baking dish from the oven, let the potatoes rest for 5 minutes, then serve.

Spinach Fettuccine Alfredo

SERVES: 4
PREPARATION TIME: 10 minutes
COOKING TIME: 3 minutes

Salt, for cooking the pasta (optional)
1 package (9 ounces) refrigerated fresh fettuccine
1 container (10 ounces) refrigerated Alfredo-style pasta sauce
1 package (10 ounces) frozen creamed spinach, thawed
1 tablespoon dry white wine or fresh lemon juice
¼ teaspoon black pepper
½ cup pre-shredded Parmesan cheese
2 tablespoons chopped fresh basil, parsley, or scallions, for garnish

BRING a large pot of water to a boil over high heat. Add salt, if using, and stir in the fettuccine. Reduce the heat to medium-high and cook the fettuccine, uncovered, until al dente, 3 minutes.
MEANWHILE, place the pasta sauce, spinach, wine, and pepper in a 2-quart saucepan and stir to combine. Bring the mixture to a boil over medium-high heat and let boil, stirring, to reduce the liquid slightly, 2 minutes. Remove the pan from the heat and cover to keep warm.
DRAIN the fettuccine well in a colander, shaking it a few times to remove any water that might still cling to the pasta. Return the fettuccine to the pot. Spoon the spinach sauce over it. Add the Parmesan cheese and stir to coat the pasta well with the sauce. Spoon onto serving plates and garnish with the basil.

15 ways to doctor frozen peas

HERE ARE SOME HOT IDEAS for making the most of frozen peas during the holidays.

1 Add a cup of frozen peas to your favorite casserole recipes for a bit of color.

2 Blend thawed peas with hot cooked basmati rice and a teaspoon of curry powder for a flavorful Indian side.

3 Cook your favorite creamy rice blend and add cooked peas and a small jar of diced pimiento.

4 Need Spanish rice? Add the thawed peas to saffron-flavored rice blends.

5 Combine a box of cooked peas with a box of cooked sugar snap peas. Add a little onion and red bell pepper that has been sautéed until softened in butter.

6 Add peas and a shot of sherry to your holiday green bean casserole. Or switch the casserole completely to peas and pearl onions topped with crunchy onions.

7 Refrigerated Alfredo sauce and peas are natural partners for pasta. Toss with fettuccine or bow ties and serve as a first coarse. Add chunks of ham or cooked shrimp for a heartier dish.

8 Here's a bright and festive sauce to serve alongside grilled salmon. Puree cooked peas with ½ cup of chicken broth and a couple of tablespoons of shallots sautéed in a couple of tablespoons of melted butter. Add a splash of heavy cream to enrich it if desired.

9 Add thawed peas to deli soups to add color and heft. Also try them in seafood chowders and bisques.

10 Add cooked peas and a box of cooked frozen artichoke hearts to deli creamed spinach. Bake in a gratin dish topped with buttered bread crumbs.

11 Add sautéed shiitake mushrooms to cooked peas for an elegant side.

12 Sprinkle cooked and buttered peas with toasted sliced almonds and shredded good Parmesan cheese before serving.

13 Toss warm, roasted new potatoes with cooked, drained peas and bottled pesto. Garnish with cherry tomato halves and sprinkle with Parmesan cheese.

14 Toss bright green thawed peas in a salad with Bibb lettuce, beets, crunchy crumbled bacon, and red onion slivers. Dress it with your favorite mustardy vinaigrette.

15 Add thawed chilled peas to deli seafood salads for a splash of color. Serve in pre-baked appetizer tart shells. Garnish with sprigs of watercress or parsley.

Stir-Fried Sweet Carrot Slices

SERVES: 3 to 4
PREPARATION TIME: 3 minutes
COOKING TIME: 4 to 5 minutes

1 tablespoon olive oil
1 package (8 ounces) pre-shredded carrots
¼ cup store-bought orange juice
2 teaspoons light brown sugar or granulated sugar
Salt
1 scallion, green part only, minced

HEAT the olive oil in a large skillet over medium heat. Stir in the carrots and cook, stirring constantly, until they soften, 2 to 3 minutes. Be careful that the carrots do not stick to the bottom of the skillet. Add the orange juice and brown sugar and season with salt to taste. Cover the skillet, reduce the heat to low, and let the carrots simmer until they soften a bit more, 2 minutes more. Sprinkle the scallions over the top and serve the carrots at once.

Mom's Broccoli and Rice Casserole

SERVES: 8 to 10
PREPARATION TIME: 15 minutes
BAKING TIME: 25 to 30 minutes

2 packages (10 ounces each) frozen chopped broccoli
Vegetable oil cooking spray, for misting the baking dish
1 cup instant rice
1 can (10.75 ounces) cream of mushroom soup
½ cup processed cheese spread, such as Cheez Whiz
⅓ cup milk
Pinch of black pepper, or dash of hot pepper sauce (optional)
½ cup pre-shredded sharp Cheddar cheese

PLACE a rack in the center of the oven and preheat the oven to 375°F.

PLACE the frozen broccoli in a microwave-safe dish and cook on high power until the broccoli thaws enough to be broken up, about 2 minutes. Mist a 13- by 9-inch (3-quart) glass or ceramic baking dish with vegetable oil cooking spray. Transfer the broccoli and its liquid to the baking dish and place in the oven to continue thawing.

PLACE the rice, mushroom soup, cheese spread, milk, and, if using, pepper in a large mixing bowl. Stir until well combined. The mixture will be thick.

REMOVE the baking dish from the oven and, using a wooden spoon, spread the broccoli evenly over the bottom of the dish. It is fine if the broccoli is still a little frozen. Spoon the rice mixture over the broccoli in an even layer. Sprinkle the Cheddar cheese on top.

RETURN the baking dish to the oven and bake the casserole until it is bubbling throughout and lightly browned around the edges, 25 to 30 minutes. Serve the casserole at once.

---

15 ways to doctor frozen mashed potatoes

FROZEN MASHED POTATOES are potato granules you combine with milk to create a luscious side. They are improved when you doctor them up with tasty additions.

1 Season the mashed potatoes with cream, butter, white pepper, and salt. Fold in shredded Gruyère cheese and top with more cheese before heating.

2 For a twice-baked casserole, blend the potatoes with milk, sour cream, butter, and crumbled bacon or country ham bits. Fold in Cheddar cheese, adding more on top. Bake and serve sprinkled with chives or sliced green onions.

3 Make an earthy potato bake with lots of sautéed mushrooms and onions. Add milk or cream and butter. Sprinkle with fresh herbs and freshly grated Parmesan cheese.

4 For horseradish-seasoned potatoes to accompany roasted beef, blend in sour cream and prepared horseradish.

5 Add more milk than the package calls for to make an easy and quick potato soup. Garnish with chives.

6 Add clams or smoked sausage to #5 for a quick and creamy clam chowder or a creamy potato soup with smoked sausage.

7 Blend good-quality unsweetened plain yogurt into the mashed potatoes. Sprinkle with toasted cumin seeds and serve with roasted lamb.

8 Form prepared mashed potatoes into cakes and pan-fry until golden. Top with sautéed green onion slices and serve with salmon or beef.

9 Drizzle mashed potatoes with a blend of olive oil, mashed garlic, and chopped fresh parsley. Serve with lamb.

10 Sauté a couple of leeks with bits of ham. Stir them into buttery mashed potatoes.

11 Fill bell pepper boats with mashed potatoes. Top with cheese—shredded Swiss, Cheddar, or Parmesan—then bake until warmed through.

12 Fold shredded pepper Jack cheese into the mashed potatoes. Serve with grilled flank steak.

13 Blend shoepeg corn into the mashed potatoes. Add plenty of butter and black pepper.

14 Add lots of fresh roasted garlic to creamy, buttery mashed potatoes. Roast whole garlic wrapped in foil in a medium oven. Poke with a knife to test for doneness. It's ready when soft (about 40 minutes at 400°F).

15 Add cream cheese to mashed potatoes if you want them to hold well for holiday buffets. Top with canned fried onions.

Sautéed Spinach with Lemon

SERVES: 4
PREPARATION TIME: 3 to 4 minutes
COOKING TIME: 3 to 5 minutes

1 small lemon
2 tablespoons olive oil
2 cloves garlic, sliced
1 bag (10 ounces) fresh spinach
Salt and black pepper

GRATE the zest of the lemon, then squeeze the juice from it. Set the lemon zest and juice aside.

HEAT the olive oil in a large skillet over medium heat. Add the garlic and cook it until it deepens in color, 1 to 2 minutes. Add the spinach to the skillet and carefully pack it down with your hand. Cook, stirring, until the spinach wilts and is tender, 2 to 3 minutes. Season the spinach with salt and pepper to taste. Add the lemon zest and juice to the spinach, stir well to mix, then serve.

Down-Home Corn

SERVES: 6
PREPARATION TIME: 5 minutes
COOKING TIME: 8 to 10 minutes

1 package (16 ounces; 3 generous cups) frozen white shoepeg corn

The Green Bean
Casserole Revisited

TRANSFORM PACKAGED STUFFING MIX into a grand holiday side by using these suggestions and your creativity.

1 **Add chopped fresh apples** and toasted pecans.

2 **Stir in a can of hominy,** ham bits, and cooked collard greens.

3 **Add sliced andouille sausage** and sautéed red and green bell peppers.

4 **Add cooked and crumbled chorizo sausage** and chopped green chiles.

5 **Add buttery sautéed onions** and mushrooms.

6 **Add corn kernels** and a small jar of pimientos.

7 **Add cooked and crumbled sage-flavored home-style pork sausage.** Fold in diced apple and celery, too.

8 **Fold in lots** of chopped fresh parsley.

9 **Add cooked and crumbled Italian sausage,** garlic, and thawed and drained chopped spinach.

10 **Add dried cranberries,** orange zest, and cooked wild rice.

11 **Flavor with apple cider** and fold in dried apples.

12 **Add sautéed leeks** and cooked ham chunks.

13 **Add chopped canned water chestnuts** and cooked pearl onions.

14 **Add a can of smoked oysters.**

15 **Add a can of baby clams,** bacon bits, buttery sautéed red bell pepper bits, and lots of fresh parsley, creating a Clams Casino Stuffing.

---

4 tablespoons (½ stick) butter
½ cup heavy (whipping) cream
2 teaspoons cornstarch
1 teaspoon sugar
Salt and black pepper
½ cup water

PLACE the corn, butter, cream, cornstarch, sugar, and salt and pepper to taste in a large skillet or 2-quart saucepan over medium heat. Add ½ cup of water and stir until the mixture just comes to a boil, making sure that the cornstarch dissolves completely. Reduce the heat to medium-low and let the mixture simmer, uncovered, stirring occasionally, until it thickens, 6 to 7 minutes more. If you want a creamier consistency, transfer the corn mixture to a food processor and pulse several times to break up the corn kernels. If you do this, reheat the corn briefly, then serve it at once.

The Green Bean Casserole Revisited

SERVES: 8
PREPARATION TIME: 12 minutes
BAKING TIME: 20 to 25 minutes

1 tablespoon butter
1 medium-size red bell pepper, sliced

1 medium-size onion, thinly sliced
1 can (10.75 ounces) reduced-fat cream of mushroom soup
½ cup milk
¼ cup sherry
1 package (16 ounces) frozen French-cut green beans
1 can (2.8 ounces; 1⅓ cups) French-fried onions
¼ cup pre-sliced almonds

PLACE a rack in the center of the oven and preheat the oven to 375°F.
MELT the butter in a large skillet over medium heat. If you use a 10-inch (3-quart) ovenproof skillet you will also be able to bake the casserole in it. Add bell pepper and the onion and cook, stirring, until soft, 3 minutes. Add the mushroom soup, milk, and sherry and continue cooking, stirring, until the mixture comes to a boil, 2 minutes. Stir in the frozen green beans. Turn off the heat and stir until the beans begin to thaw. If you are not baking the casserole in the skillet, transfer it to a 13- by 9-inch (3-quart) glass or ceramic baking dish that's been misted with vegetable oil cooking spray. Top with the French-fried onions and almonds.
BAKE the casserole until it is bubbling throughout and the French-fried onions and almonds are browned, 20 to 25 minutes. Serve at once.

Pumpkin-Orange
Soup with
Parmesan Toasts

Soup, Salad, and Sandwich Sampler

Serve up a tasty dinner with these superb soups, sensational salads, and clever sandwiches.

Pumpkin-Orange Soup with Parmesan Toasts

SERVES: 6 to 8 as an appetizer
PREPARATION TIME: 10 minutes
COOKING TIME: 8 to 10 minutes

1 can (15 ounces) pumpkin
2 cans (14 to 14.5 ounces each) low-sodium chicken broth
1 clove garlic, crushed in a garlic press
1 bay leaf
1 teaspoon dried thyme
1 medium-size orange, rinsed
8 slices (½-inch thick) French bread
1 tablespoon olive oil
2 tablespoons grated Parmesan cheese

PREHEAT the broiler.

PLACE the pumpkin, broth, garlic, bay leaf, and thyme in a 2-quart saucepan; heat over medium-high heat, stirring just to combine. While the mixture is coming to a boil, grate 1 teaspoon orange zest for and add this to the soup. Cut the orange in half and juice it; you should have ⅓ cup. Stir the orange juice into the soup. When the soup comes to a boil, cover the pan and reduce the heat to low. Let simmer, stirring soup occasionally, until it is thickened and the flavors blend, 8 minutes.

MEANWHILE, make the Parmesan toasts: Place the slices of bread on a baking sheet and broil them until they are lightly browned, 1 minute. Remove the baking sheet from the broiler, turn the bread slices over, brush the untoasted side with the olive oil, and sprinkle some of the Parmesan cheese

(continued on page 72)

15 ways to doctor canned soup

1 Tomato soup turns into a sweet and tangy grilled chicken marinade by adding a little Worcestershire sauce, vinegar, brown sugar, and chopped onion. Let chicken pieces marinate overnight, then cook over a low fire.

2 Remember those marinated carrots called copper pennies? You combine a can of tomato soup, a cup of sugar, ¼ cup of vegetable oil, Worcestershire sauce, and mustard to taste. Pour over from 3 to 4 cups of sliced and drained canned carrots and refrigerate overnight.

3 Turn tomato soup into a delicacy by adding a little heavy (whipping) cream, chopped fresh basil, chopped fresh tomatoes, black pepper, and a splash of vodka.

4 Combine cream of mushroom soup with a can of milk, a package of sliced mushrooms that you lightly sauté in butter, and browned chicken pieces. Cover and bake at 325°F for 1½ hours or until tender.

5 Add cream of mushroom soup to your favorite spaghetti sauce recipe. Fold in cooked spaghetti, then briefly bake for a creamy pasta casserole.

6 For an impromptu bean dip, pour a can of chili with beans into a small casserole. Top with shredded Cheddar cheese and chopped onion and bake until bubbly. Serve with tortilla chips and salsa.

7 Heat vegetable soup, add a dash of hot pepper sauce, and stir in a small can of crabmeat for a tangy crab stew.

8 Use cream of chicken soup as a base for chicken potpie. Add 1 to 2 cups of chopped chicken and a couple of cups of frozen vegetables per can of soup. Thin as needed with canned chicken broth. Fold into a thawed frozen deep-dish pie crust and top with strips of thawed pastry. Bake at 350°F until golden and bubbly.

9 Add a handful of chopped fresh broccoli to a can of cream of broccoli soup and heat as directed. Season with chopped onion and black pepper.

10 Thin a can of cream of broccoli soup with a little milk. Pour over a couple of cups of sliced turkey and a cup of thawed chopped broccoli in a casserole. Sprinkle with Parmesan cheese and buttered bread crumbs and bake at 400°F until bubbly.

11 Who can forget classic tuna noodle casserole? Cook 1½ cups of egg noodles. Drain and combine with a can of drained tuna, a can of cream of mushroom soup, and a cup of milk. Season as desired, top with bread crumbs, and bake at 350°F for 30 minutes, or until bubbly.

12 Open a can of split pea soup, add canned chicken broth instead of water, and add a splash of sherry. Simmer uncovered until bubbly.

13 Heat a can of onion soup as directed, adding sherry to taste. Pour into serving bowls and top with toasted slices of French bread covered in melted Parmesan cheese and chopped fresh parsley.

14 Don't forget canned chicken broth. Open a can and add a handful of your favorite pasta (uncooked), a handful of frozen peas, and a tablespoon of chopped onion. Season as desired and cook until the pasta is done for a fresh and light chicken soup.

15 Beef broth can transform ordinary rice. Cook your favorite rice in beef broth and, when done, fold in sautéed mushrooms.

15 ways to doctor bagged salad greens

SO MANY CHOICES ARE IN THE SUPER-MARKET CASE: baby greens, chopped romaine, iceberg, and fancy European mixes. Remember that the best salads don't overdo ingredients; keep it simple but interesting.

1 **Toss baby greens with yellow bell pepper strips and slivers of red cabbage.** Dress with your favorite vinaigrette.

2 **Turn those greens elegantly Asian by adding a sweet rice wine vinaigrette,** thinly sliced seedless cucumber, fresh cilantro, and chopped peanuts.

3 **Add classic holiday color with blanched sugar snap peas or pea pods and red bell pepper strips.** Dress with a balsamic vinaigrette.

4 **Add drained canned beets cut into chunks, fresh green apple chunks, and crispy crumbled bacon.** Toss with a mustardy vinaigrette.

5 **Dried cranberries, orange segments, and toasted pecans are festive for the holidays.** Dress with a sweet but tangy poppy seed vinaigrette.

6 **Arrange canned pear halves (or thinly sliced fresh Bosc pear) over greens** with crumbled blue cheese and pomegranate seeds. Dress with vinaigrette.

7 **Add beautifully ripe avocado slices and grapefruit segments** (available in a jar in the produce section). Dress with a peppery vinaigrette.

8 **Turn a bag of salad into a holiday Cobb or chef salad with chunks of roast turkey and ham.** Now add whatever you like: blue or Cheddar cheese, hard-cooked eggs, chopped fresh apple, toasted nuts, or dried cranberries. Dress with good ol' Thousand Island or a vinaigrette.

9 **Add a small bag of shredded carrots** to any bag of mixed salad greens. It's a healthy and colorful addition.

10 **Take advantage of peppery radishes and watercress.** Add rounds of radishes and sprigs of watercress to baby romaine. This is especially delicious if roasted beef and potatoes are on the menu.

11 **Potato salad doesn't have to be reserved for warm weather only.** Toss leftover roasted potatoes with bottled Caesar vinaigrette and pile on top of salad greens. Add your favorite potato salad add-tos, such as celery, bell pepper, olives, and hard-cooked egg. Add a handful of crumbled country ham if you've got it.

12 **Turn those greens into a Greek salad** with a drained can of chickpeas, sliced celery, red onion, and lemony vinaigrette. Top with crumbled feta cheese and a few Greek olives.

13 **No dressing in the fridge?** Make a homemade Thousand Island by combining mayo with chili sauce (or ketchup in a pinch) and a spoonful of sweet or dill pickle relish. Spoon over chopped iceberg lettuce.

14 **Here's an old classic: wilted salad.** Fry a few slices of bacon, crumble, and reserve. Add a couple tablespoons of cider vinegar and a spoonful of sugar to the warm drippings and pour over a bag of baby greens. Top with crumbled bacon, minced onion, and crumbed hard-cooked egg.

15 **Add toasted pumpkin seeds, sliced green onions, and chopped cilantro.** Toss with a vinaigrette enhanced with a spoonful of salsa. Or pick a bottled Southwestern-style vinaigrette with lime juice.

over each slice, dividing it equally among them. Return the bread slices to the broiler and broil until the Parmesan melts, 15 to 20 seconds. Remove the baking sheet from the broiler and keep the toasts warm until ready to serve.

TO serve, remove and discard the bay leaf from the soup. Ladle the soup into serving bowls and top each with toasts or pass the toasts separately.

Taco Soup

SERVES: 4 to 6 as a main course
PREPARATION TIME: 10 minutes
COOKING TIME: 20 to 22 minutes

Olive oil cooking spray
½ pound ground beef round
1 cup chopped onion (from 1 medium-size onion)
1 can (14.5 ounces) Mexican-style diced tomatoes, with their liquid
1 can (15.5 ounces) light red kidney beans, with their liquid
1 can (11 ounces) corn kernels, with their liquid
1 can (8 ounces) tomato sauce
1 package (1.25 ounces) reduced-sodium taco seasoning
1 avocado, peeled and cubed
1 cup sour cream
1 cup pre-shredded Cheddar or Monterey Jack cheese
¼ cup fresh cilantro sprigs
1 lime, halved and cut into 4 wedges
Tortilla chips

SPRAY a 4-quart saucepan with olive oil cooking spray and place it over medium-high heat. Crumble in the ground beef and break it up with a wooden spoon, then cook, stirring, 30 seconds. Add the onion and, continuing to stir, cook until the beef browns all over and is cooked through and the onion softens, 3 to 4 minutes. Stir in the tomatoes, beans, and corn with their liquids, tomato sauce, and taco seasoning. Fill the tomato sauce can with water, add this to the pan, and stir. Bring to a boil, then reduce the heat to low, cover the pan, and let simmer 15 minutes.

LADLE the hot soup into serving bowls and pass the avocado cubes, sour cream, cheese, cilantro, lime wedges, and tortilla chips separately.

Creamy Potato Soup

SERVES: 4 as a main course
PREPARATION TIME: 5 minutes
COOKING TIME: 10 minutes

4 cups frozen mashed potatoes, such
  as Ore-Ida Just Add Milk
2 cups milk
1 can (14 to 14.5 ounces) chicken broth
1 tablespoon butter (optional)
Pre-grated Cheddar cheese, chopped
  scallion, snipped chives, crumbled
  bacon, and/or black pepper, for
  garnish

PLACE the frozen mashed potatoes, milk, and chicken broth in a 2-quart saucepan and bring to a boil, stirring, over medium-high heat. Then reduce the heat to low, cover the pan, and let the soup simmer until creamy, 8 minutes, stirring frequently.

REMOVE the pan from the heat, stir in the butter, if using, and ladle the soup into serving bowls. Garnish with the topping(s) of your choice.

Winter's Night Beef Stew

SERVES: 4 to 6 as a main course
PREPARATION TIME: 8 minutes
COOKING TIME: 25 to 26 minutes

1 tablespoon vegetable oil
1 pound pre-cut lean beef cubes
  (½-inch cubes)
1 medium-size onion, thinly sliced
1 tablespoon all-purpose flour
¼ teaspoon black pepper
1 can (14 to 14.5 ounces) beef broth
1 can (10.75 ounces) beef stew
1 medium-size turnip, chopped
1 cup chopped carrots
1 bay leaf
1 tablespoon Madeira, sherry, or red
  wine (optional)

HEAT the oil in a large pot over medium-high heat. Add the beef cubes and cook, stirring occasionally, until well browned on all sides, 3 to 4 minutes. Add the onion and cook, stirring, until the onion softens, 2 minutes more. Add the flour and pepper and stir to coat the beef. Add the beef broth, canned beef stew, turnip, carrots, bay leaf, and, if using,

Warm Arugula Salad
with Roasted Asparagus

Madeira. Bring the mixture to a boil and cook for 2 minutes, then reduce the heat to low, cover the pot, and let simmer until the turnip and carrots are cooked through, 18 minutes more.

TO serve, remove and discard the bay leaf. Ladle the stew into serving bowls.

Blue Cheese, Walnut, and Apple Slaw

SERVES: 6 to 8 as a side dish
PREPARATION TIME: 10 to 12 minutes

⅓ cup walnut pieces
1 medium-size apple
½ cup bottled Ranch salad dressing
¼ cup pre-crumbled blue cheese
1 bag (16 ounces) coleslaw mix
Black pepper

PREHEAT the oven to 350°F.
PLACE the walnut pieces on a rimmed baking sheet and bake them until they begin to darken, 5 to 7 minutes.
MEANWHILE, coarsely grate the apple using the side of a box grater with the largest holes; you should have about 1 cup.
PLACE the dressing and blue cheese in a large serving bowl. Stir to combine and

mash the cheese a bit to incorporate it into the dressing. Add the coleslaw mix and grated apple and stir to coat it well with the dressing. Season with pepper to taste. Just before serving, sprinkle toasted walnuts on top of the slaw.

Warm Arugula Salad with Roasted Asparagus

SERVES: 4 as a starter or side dish
PREPARATION TIME: 15 minutes
BAKING TIME: 5 to 6 minutes

1 bunch of thin asparagus (about
  30 stalks)
2 tablespoons olive oil
Salt
⅓ cup bottled balsamic vinaigrette
½ cup store-bought roasted red
  pepper strips
¼ cup pitted Kalamata olives
4 cups prewashed baby arugula,
  trimmed and leaves torn into pieces

PREHEAT the oven to 400°F.
RINSE the asparagus spears, pat dry, and snap off and discard the tough ends. Place the asparagus in a shallow baking pan, drizzle with the olive oil,

(continued on page 74)

and sprinkle with salt to taste. Bake the asparagus until it just begins to take on a roasted appearance, 5 to 6 minutes.

MEANWHILE, warm the balsamic vinaigrette in a small saucepan over low heat. Do not let it come to a boil.

REMOVE the baking pan from the oven and toss the red pepper strips and olives with the hot asparagus. Either divide the arugula among four salad plates or place the arugula in a medium-size salad bowl. Top it with the asparagus mixture. Spoon the warmed dressing over the salad and serve at once.

Susan's Penne and Grape Tomato Salad

SERVES: 6 to 8 as a main course
PREPARATION TIME: 15 minutes

Salt, for cooking the pasta (optional)
1 pound penne, uncooked
1 bag (6 ounces) fresh spinach
1 pint grape tomatoes
½ cup bottled balsamic vinaigrette, or more if needed
1 package (4 ounces) pre-crumbled basil and tomato feta cheese
½ cup fresh basil slivers

BRING a large pot of water to a boil over high heat. Add salt, if using, and stir in the penne. Reduce the heat to medium-high and cook the penne uncovered, until al dente, 8 to 10 minutes.

MEANWHILE, chop the spinach and cut the tomatoes in half.

DRAIN the penne well in a colander, shaking it a few times to remove any water that might still cling to the pasta. Transfer the penne to a serving bowl and pour the vinaigrette over it. Stir to combine. Fold in the chopped spinach, tomato halves, and feta cheese. Stir until all of the ingredients are coated with vinaigrette. Add more vinaigrette if needed to moisten the salad. Sprinkle the basil over the top of the salad and serve at once; or cover the bowl with plastic wrap and refrigerate it for up to 24 hours.

Mom's Potato Salad

SERVES: 6 to 8 as a side dish
PREPARATION TIME: 25 minutes

2½ pounds new potatoes
Pinch of salt
1 package (10 ounces) frozen peas
1 cup finely chopped celery (from 1 to 2 ribs)
½ cup chopped scallions, both white and light green parts (from 4 scallions)
1 envelope (0.7 ounce) Good Seasons Italian salad dressing mix
⅓ cup olive oil

RINSE the potatoes well under running water and scrub them to remove any dirt. Cut larger potatoes into eighths; cut smaller potatoes into quarters. Place the potatoes in a 4-quart saucepan and cover them with cold water, then add the salt. Place the pan over high heat, cover it, and bring to a boil. When the water is boiling, reduce the heat to low and let the potatoes simmer, covered, until they are just tender when tested with a fork, 10 minutes. Pour off the water and place the potatoes on a work surface to cool for 10 minutes.

MEANWHILE, place the frozen peas, celery, scallions, and salad dressing mix in a large serving bowl and stir to combine.

WHEN the potatoes are cool enough to handle (but still quite warm), remove the skins and cut each potato into about 1-inch cubes. Add the cubed potatoes to the bowl with the peas and toss (the warmth of the potatoes will thaw the frozen peas). Pour the olive oil over the salad and stir with a large spoon to combine well, making sure that all of the potatoes are coated with olive oil. Serve the salad at once or cover the bowl with plastic wrap and refrigerate it for up to 3 days.

New-Fashioned Pimiento Cheese

SERVES: 4 to 6
PREPARATION TIME: 5 to 7 minutes

1 package (8 ounces; 2 cups) pre-shredded sharp Cheddar cheese
1 jar (2 ounces) diced or sliced pimiento peppers, drained
1 tablespoon minced onion
Dash of Worcestershire sauce
¼ cup mayonnaise
Black pepper
Soda crackers or thin slices of toasted French bread, for serving

PLACE the Cheddar cheese, pimientos, onion, and Worcestershire sauce in a small glass bowl and stir to combine.

FOLD in the mayonnaise and stir until everything is well blended. Season with pepper to taste.

PLACE the bowl on a serving platter and surround it with soda crackers or

---

5 great ways to use a spoonful of pimiento cheese

1 **Spread it** on half an English muffin and run this under the broiler until the cheese bubbles.

2 **Dollop it** generously on a burger hot off the grill.

3 **Tuck it** inside a hot baked potato.

4 **Add some** pimiento cheese to a toasted BLT.

5 **Sandwich it** between two slices of bread and sauté the sandwich in melted butter, turning once to toast both sides, for a change of pace from the usual grilled cheese.

Chicken Fajita Wraps

PREHEAT the oven to 350°F.

WRAP the tortillas in aluminum foil so that they are completely covered and place them in the oven.

PLACE the olive oil in a large skillet over medium-high heat. While it is heating, toss the chicken and fajita seasoning together in a bowl, stirring to coat the chicken well.

SPOON the coated chicken slices into the hot oil and cook on all sides, until it is fully cooked, 4 to 5 minutes, reducing the heat to medium if the chicken is browning too fast. Add the beans and corn and cook, stirring, until heated through, 1 to 2 minutes. Add the cheese and let simmer just until it begins to melt, 1 minute more. Turn off the heat.

REMOVE the tortillas from the oven. Place a tortilla on a work surface and spoon some of the chicken mixture evenly down the center. Roll the tortilla up tightly. Repeat with the remaining tortillas and filling. Serve at once with the salsa.

Mini Cheese Calzones

SERVES: 6 (makes 12 mini calzones)
PREPARATION TIME: 15 minutes
BAKING TIME: 12 minutes

6 sticks (1 ounce each) string cheese
1 package (11 ounces) refrigerated
　　bread-stick dough
1 cup jarred marinara sauce or pizza
　　sauce, for serving

PREHEAT the oven to 400°F.

UNWRAP the string cheese sticks and cut them in half crosswise. Open or unroll the bread-stick dough and separate it into 12 rectangles. Coil a rectangle of bread-stick dough around a piece of cheese stick as if you were wrapping it with yarn. Completely cover the cheese, tucking the dough ends under and pinching them to seal closed. Repeat with the remaining dough and cheese. Place the dough-covered cheese on an ungreased baking sheet.

BAKE the mini calzones until they are golden brown, about 12 minutes. Remove them from the baking sheet and serve at once with a bowl of marinara or pizza sauce for dunking.

French bread toasts. If you are making the pimiento cheese ahead, cover the bowl with plastic wrap and chill until serving, then remove it from the refrigerator 30 minutes before serving to allow the flavors to develop.

Pesto Focaccia Sandwich

SERVES: 6
PREPARATION TIME: 10 minutes
BAKING TIME: 10 minutes

1 large deli-loaf focaccia or ciabatta
　　bread
1 jar (3.5 ounces) prepared pesto
　　sauce
½ pound thinly sliced Black Forest
　　ham
½ pound thinly sliced roasted turkey
　　breast
6 provolone cheese slices
½ small red onion, thinly sliced

PREHEAT the oven to 450°F. Cut the bread in half horizontally using a serrated knife. Spread the pesto sauce evenly over the cut sides of the bread. Layer ham, turkey, cheese, and onion slices evenly over bottom half of the bread. Top with remaining bread half and wrap in aluminum foil.

BAKE the sandwich for 10 minutes. Cut into six wedges to serve.

Chicken Fajita Wraps

SERVES: 12 as an appetizer, 6 as a main
　　course
PREPARATION TIME: 12 minutes

6 flour tortillas (10 inches each)
1 tablespoon olive oil
1 pound skinless, boneless chicken
　　breasts, cut into ½-inch slices
1 package (1.12 ounces) fajita
　　seasoning mix
1 can (15 to 16 ounces) black or pinto
　　beans, drained
1 can (11 ounces) yellow corn with
　　red and green peppers, drained
1 package (8 ounces; 2 cups)
　　pre-shredded Monterey Jack
　　cheese with jalapeño peppers
1 jar of your favorite chunky
　　salsa

Santa's Bread Shoppe

Even if you've never baked bread before, these easy recipes make you feel like a pro.

Bread Sticks Three Ways

MAKES: 1 dozen
PREPARATION TIME: 12 minutes
BAKING TIME: 15 to 20 minutes

1 package (11 ounces) refrigerated
   plain bread stick dough

Garlic and Fennel Topping
1 tablespoon olive oil
2 cloves garlic, crushed in a garlic
   press
1 teaspoon fennel seeds
Coarse salt

Poppy Seed and Paprika Topping
1 tablespoon olive oil
1 teaspoon poppy seeds
Paprika
Seasoned salt

Cheddar and Chive Topping
¼ cup pre-shredded sharp Cheddar
   cheese
1 tablespoon minced fresh chives

PLACE a rack in the center of the oven and preheat the oven to 375°F.
UNROLL the bread stick dough and separate it into 12 pieces. Place the strips of dough on an ungreased baking sheet.
FOR GARLIC AND FENNEL TOPPING: Brush four strips of dough with 1 tablespoon of olive oil. Sprinkle the garlic and fennel seeds over these strips of dough, dividing them evenly among them. Season these bread sticks with coarse salt.
FOR POPPY SEED AND PAPRIKA TOPPING: Brush four more strips of dough with 1 tablespoon of olive oil. Sprinkle the poppy seeds over the strips, dividing them evenly among them. Season with paprika and seasoned salt.
FOR CHEDDAR AND CHIVE TOPPING: Sprinkle the remaining four strips of dough with the Cheddar cheese and chives, dividing them evenly among them.

BAKE the bread sticks until they are golden brown, 15 to 20 minutes. Using a metal spatula, transfer the bread sticks to a serving plate and serve at once.

Tomato and Feta Focaccia

MAKES: 1 focaccia
PREPARATION TIME: 15 minutes
BAKING TIME: 15 to 18 minutes

1 package (10 ounces) refrigerated
   pizza crust dough
2 tablespoons olive oil
3 cloves garlic, crushed in a garlic press
⅓ cup pre-crumbled feta cheese
   (optional)
½ cup thinly sliced tomato (from
   1 medium-size tomato)
Coarse salt

PLACE a rack in the center of the oven and preheat the oven to 400°F.
UNROLL the dough onto an ungreased rimmed baking sheet. Using your hands, form the dough into an 11- by 7-inch rectangle. With your fingertips, make indentations all over the dough. Drizzle the olive oil evenly over the dough. Scatter the garlic and, if using, feta cheese over the dough. Arrange the tomato slices evenly on top of the dough. Season the tomatoes with salt.
BAKE the focaccia until it is golden brown, 15 to 18 minutes. Remove the pan from the oven and, when the focaccia is cool enough to handle, cut it into squares, using a pizza cutter. Serve the focaccia with dinner or drinks.

Scallion and Cheddar Supper Bread

MAKES: 1 loaf
PREPARATION TIME: 15 minutes
BAKING TIME: 16 to 18 minutes

Vegetable oil cooking spray, for
   misting the pan
1½ cups biscuit mix, such as Bisquick
½ cup milk
1 large egg
1 cup pre-shredded sharp Cheddar
   cheese
4 scallions, both white and light green
   parts, chopped (for ½ cup)
¼ teaspoon black pepper
1 tablespoon olive oil

PLACE a rack in the center of the oven and preheat the oven to 400°F.
LIGHTLY mist an 8-inch round or square cake pan with vegetable oil cooking spray. Set the cake pan aside.
PLACE the biscuit mix, milk, and egg in a large mixing bowl and stir to just combine. Add the Cheddar cheese, scallions, and pepper and stir until all the ingredients are just incorporated. Scrape the dough into the prepared cake pan. Press it lightly with a spatula so that it reaches the sides of the pan. Drizzle the olive oil over the top.
BAKE the bread until it is golden brown and springs back when lightly pressed with a finger, 16 to 18 minutes. Remove the pan from the oven and place it on a wire rack to cool for 5 minutes, then slice the bread into squares and serve at once.

Ripe Banana Loaves

MAKES: 2 (9-inch) loaves
PREPARATION TIME: 10 minutes
BAKING TIME: 40 to 45 minutes

Solid vegetable shortening, for
   greasing the pans
Flour, for dusting the pans
1 package (18.25 ounces) plain yellow
   cake mix
½ cup packed light brown sugar
2 very ripe medium-size bananas,
   peeled and mashed (about 1 cup)
¾ cup buttermilk
½ cup vegetable oil, such as canola, corn,
   safflower, soybean, or sunflower
3 large eggs
1 teaspoon ground cinnamon

PLACE a rack in the center of the oven and preheat the oven to 350°F. Lightly

Butterscotch-Pecan Focaccia

grease two 9-inch loaf pans with vegetable shortening, then dust with flour. Shake out the excess flour. Set aside.

PLACE the cake mix, brown sugar, mashed bananas, buttermilk, oil, eggs, and cinnamon in a large mixing bowl. Blend with an electric mixer on low speed for 1 minute. Stop the machine and scrape down the sides of the bowl with a rubber spatula. Increase the mixer speed to medium and beat 2 minutes more, scraping down the sides again if needed. The batter should look well blended, and the bananas should be well pureed. Divide the batter between the prepared pans and place them side by side in the oven.

BAKE the loaves until they are golden brown and a toothpick inserted in the center of each loaf comes out clean, 40 to 45 minutes. Remove the pans from the oven and place them on wire racks to cool for 20 minutes. Run a dinner knife around the edge of each pan and invert each loaf onto a rack to cool on its side for 30 minutes more. Slice and serve.

NOTE: Store the loaves, covered in aluminum foil, at room temperature for up to 1 week. Or freeze them, wrapped in foil, for up to 6 months; thaw the loaves overnight on the counter before serving.

Butterscotch-Pecan Focaccia

MAKES: 1 focaccia
PREPARATION TIME: 15 to 20 minutes
BAKING TIME: 15 to 18 minutes

1 package (10 ounces) refrigerated pizza crust dough
2 tablespoons (¼ stick) melted butter
½ cup butterscotch chips
¼ cup firmly packed light brown sugar
¼ cup finely chopped pecans

PLACE a rack in the center of the oven and preheat the oven to 400°F.

UNROLL the dough onto an ungreased rimmed baking sheet. Using your hands, form the dough into an 11- by 7-inch rectangle. With your fingertips, make indentations all over the dough. Drizzle the melted butter evenly over the dough. Scatter the butterscotch chips, brown sugar, and pecans on top.

BAKE the focaccia until it is golden brown, 15 to 18 minutes. Remove the pan from the oven and, when the focaccia is cool enough to handle, cut it into squares, using a pizza cutter, and serve.

Big Bad Chocolate Muffins

MAKES: 18 muffins
PREPARATION TIME: 10 minutes
BAKING TIME: 20 to 24 minutes

Vegetable oil cooking spray, for misting the pans
1 package (18.25 ounces) plain devil's food cake mix
1 package (3.9 ounces) instant chocolate pudding mix
1 container (6 ounces; ¾ cup) low-fat vanilla yogurt
¾ cup water
½ cup vegetable oil
3 large eggs
2 cups semisweet chocolate chips

PLACE a rack in the center of the oven and preheat the oven to 400°F. Mist the bottom of 18 muffin cups with the vegetable oil cooking spray. Set the pans aside.

PLACE the cake mix and pudding mix in a large mixing bowl and make a well in the center. Place the yogurt, water, oil, and eggs in a small mixing bowl and stir with a fork to break up the yolks. Pour the yogurt mixture into the well of the muffin mix. Stir the ingredients together with a wooden spoon to just combine, 30 strokes. Fold in the chocolate chips and stir until just combined, another 10 strokes. The batter will be smooth. Spoon ⅓ cup batter into each prepared muffin cup, filling it three-quarters full. Place the pans in the oven.

BAKE the muffins until they just spring back when lightly pressed with your finger, 20 to 24 minutes. Remove the pans from the oven and place them on a wire rack to cool for 5 minutes. Run a dinner knife around the edges of the muffins, lift them up from the bottoms of the cups using the end of the knife, and pick them out of the cups carefully with your fingertips. Place them on a wire rack to cool for 15 minutes.

NOTE: Store these muffins, in a cake saver or under a glass dome, at room temperature for up to 5 days. Or freeze them, wrapped in aluminum foil or in a cake saver, for up to 6 months; thaw the muffins overnight in the refrigerator before serving.

Mexican Skillet Corn Bread

White Chocolate Muffins with Cinnamon Streusel

MAKES: 2 dozen
PREPARATION TIME: 15 minutes
BAKING TIME: 20 to 25 minutes

24 paper liners for muffin pans
    (2½-inch size)
6 ounces white chocolate, coarsely
    chopped
6 tablespoons (¾ stick) butter
1 package (18.25 ounces) plain white
    cake mix
¾ cup milk
3 large eggs
1 teaspoon pure vanilla extract
⅓ cup finely chopped pecans
1 tablespoon light brown sugar
½ teaspoon ground cinnamon

PLACE a rack in the center of the oven and preheat the oven to 350°F. Line 24 muffin cups with paper liners. Set the pans aside.

PLACE the white chocolate and the butter in a small saucepan over low heat. Stir constantly until both melt and the mixture is smooth, 3 to 4 minutes. Allow to cool slightly.

PLACE the cake mix, milk, eggs, vanilla, and white chocolate mixture in a large mixing bowl. Blend with an electric mixer on low speed for 1 minute. Stop the machine and scrape down the sides of the bowl with a rubber spatula. Increase the mixer speed to medium and beat 2 minutes more, scraping down the sides again if needed. The batter should look thick and well combined. Set the batter aside.

FOR the streusel, combine the pecans, brown sugar, and cinnamon in a small bowl. Stir well.

SPOON the batter into the lined muffin cups, filling each liner no more than two-thirds full. Sprinkle ½ teaspoon of the streusel mixture on top of each muffin. Place the pans in the oven.

BAKE the muffins until they spring back when lightly pressed with your finger and a toothpick inserted in the center comes out clean, 20 to 25 minutes. Remove the pans from the oven and place them on wire racks to cool for 5 minutes. Run a dinner knife around the edges of the muffin liners, lift the

To me, nothing makes a more comforting or suitable accompaniment to a pot of chili or a thick soup than just-baked corn bread.

Mexican Skillet Corn Bread

MAKES: 10 servings
PREPARATION TIME: 15 to 20 minutes
BAKING TIME: 20 to 22 minutes

1 tablespoon vegetable oil
2 packages (6.5 ounces each) corn
    bread mix
2 large eggs
1½ cups buttermilk
1 can (4.5 ounces) chopped green
    chiles, with their liquid
1 cup pre-shredded Mexican-style
    cheese
Butter, for serving

PLACE a rack in the center of the oven and preheat the oven to 450°F. Pour the oil into a 10- or 10½-inch cast-iron skillet and place the skillet in the oven while it preheats.

PLACE the corn bread mix, eggs, buttermilk, chiles with their liquid, and cheese in a large mixing bowl and stir just to combine. When the oven temperature reaches 375°F (if you don't have an oven thermometer, that should take 10 to 15 minutes) carefully remove the hot skillet. Pour the batter into the skillet and smooth the top. Return the skillet to the oven immediately. Keep the oven set to 450°F.

BAKE the corn bread until it is golden brown and springs back when lightly pressed with a finger, 20 to 22 minutes. Carefully remove the corn bread from the oven and run a knife around the edge of the corn bread to loosen it, then invert it onto a plate. Invert the corn bread again on a cutting board so that it is right side up. Slice the corn bread into wedges while hot and serve with butter.

muffins up from the bottom of the pan using the end of the knife, and pick them out carefully with your fingertips. Place them on a wire rack to cool for 15 minutes before serving.

NOTE: Store the muffins, wrapped in aluminum foil or plastic wrap, or in a cake saver, at room temperature for up to 1 week. Or freeze them, wrapped in foil, for up to 6 months; thaw the muffins overnight on the counter before serving.

15 ways to doctor refrigerated bread dough

SO MANY COMPLICATED BREAD RECIPES CAN BE MADE SIMPLER by substituting refrigerated bread dough. Here are some especially festive ideas for the holidays.

1 Spread refrigerated crescent triangles with prepared fillings available on the baking aisle: poppy seeds, plum jam, almond paste, chocolate chips, or butterscotch chips. Roll up and bake as directed, then drizzle with a little glaze made by stirring milk into confectioners' sugar.

2 To make a wreath of sweet rolls, spread out refrigerated pizza dough (or crescent dough in one large rectangle; pinch seams together). Spread with softened butter. Sprinkle with cinnamon sugar, pecans, and raisins. Roll up the dough into a log, then bring the ends of the log together to make a circle on a baking sheet; partially cut into about 8 to 10 sections. Twist each roll facing out. Brush with a little beaten egg and bake. Drizzle with a glaze of milk and confectioners' sugar.

3 Or create a savory wreath I call a wreath calzone. Roll up pizza dough with ricotta cheese, shredded mozzarella, and slices of salami or chunks of pepperoni. Form a circle and pinch to seal. Cut vertical slits in the dough. Brush with beaten egg, top with sesame seeds, and bake until golden.

4 Let a food wreath take on Mexican flavors by filling a ring of crescent dough with seasoned ground beef mixture like you would use for tacos. Fold the crescent dough up and over the filling, then bake and serve with shredded lettuce, chopped tomatoes, shredded cheese, cilantro, and limes.

5 How about pizza dough bread sticks? Cut pizza dough into 1-inch wide strips. Twist each strip and lay it on a lightly greased baking sheet. Brush with beaten egg, sprinkle with caraway seeds, Parmesan cheese, coarse salt, seasoned salt, or sesame seeds. Bake until golden brown.

6 Cut crescent roll triangles in half, forming long skinny triangles. Bake the triangles flat on a baking sheet. Brush with olive oil. Sprinkle with garlic salt, black pepper, Parmesan cheese, and Italian seasonings. Serve with cocktails or on a holiday buffet. They look fun peeking out of a bread basket.

7 Make your own focaccia with pizza dough. Drizzle with olive oil, fresh minced garlic, herbs, and Parmesan cheese. Add sliced black olives if desired. Bake and cut into small squares.

8 Use refrigerated biscuits to top a quick fruit cobbler. Make the biscuits seem more homemade by dipping first in melted butter and cinnamon sugar before topping the fruit pie filling or sweetened fresh fruits. Or cut them into quarters, dip in butter, and arrange them all over the cobbler. Sprinkle with cinnamon sugar, then bake.

9 Make your own biscuit cups for holding sweet or savory things. Press refrigerated biscuits into greased muffin cups, pressing the dough up the sides. Spoon in a filling before baking. For savory fillings, try generous spoonfuls of chili, creamed chicken, or spinach. For sweet fillings, add a cheesecake filling made from 8 ounces cream cheese, 1 egg, and ¼ cup of sugar, plus vanilla.

10 Make mini meatball Wellingtons. Wrap frozen and thawed meatballs with biscuit dough rolled out into larger thin circles. Pinch the dough together and place on a baking sheet. Bake until golden brown and the meatballs are warmed through. Serve on a kids' buffet table with ketchup for dipping.

11 Divide crescent dough into two rectangles. Spread one rectangle on a baking sheet. Blend ¼ cup of melted butter with ½ cup of sugar and a cup of ground almonds, walnuts or pecans. Spread over the crescent rectangle. Top with the other crescent rectangle. Brush the top with melted butter and sprinkle with sugar. Bake until golden brown. Cut into slivers to serve.

12 Place refrigerated biscuits in a buttered 8-inch square baking pan. They'll be packed in tightly. Drizzle with ¼ cup of butter and sprinkle with a couple of tablespoons of sesame seeds. Bake until golden for a fun pull-apart biscuit bread.

13 For a sweeter version, more like biscuit monkey bread, cut biscuits into quarters. Dip in melted butter. Layer in a Bundt or tube pan with cinnamon sugar, raisins, and nuts. For a savory monkey bread, layer the buttered biscuit balls with Parmesan cheese and a sprinkling of chopped fresh herbs.

14 Lay crescent dough over your favorite chicken potpie or other main-dish casserole recipe instead of pastry. Brush with beaten egg before baking.

15 Make easy coffee cake rings with biscuit dough in a Bundt or tube pan. Layer biscuits with melted butter and plenty of sugar. Add whatever you like as you go—cinnamon, candied fruits, dried fruits, nuts—and bake until golden. Unmold, allow to cool, then slice.

Deli-icious Secrets!

For spur-of-the-moment meals—or even meals planned in advance—
the supermarket deli counter can be a lifesaver.

15 ways to doctor deli chicken salad

1 **Blend in crumbled blue cheese** and almonds or toasted sesame seeds. Garnish with sliced fresh strawberries.

2 **Include toasted walnuts,** chopped red or green apple, raisins, and sliced celery for Waldorf Chicken Salad.

3 **Accent with chunks of canned or fresh pineapple** and slivered almonds.

4 **Serve with chopped fresh parsley** and Kalamata olives.

5 **Incorporate red grape halves** and toasted chopped pecans.

6 **Add 1 or 2 spoonfuls of jarred pesto** and chopped red bell pepper.

7 **Add a spoonful of mango chutney** and a smidgen of curry powder.

8 **Incorporate green onion slices** and a handful of finely chopped country ham or bacon.

9 **Add finely sliced pea pods** and thawed green peas.

10 **Add chopped cilantro leaves,** a squeeze of lime juice, and a minced chipotle pepper.

11 **Boost with a spoonful of jarred chopped olive salad.**

12 **Accent with finely chopped sweet Vidalia onion,** fresh lemon zest, and a few capers.

13 **Blend in shredded sharp Cheddar cheese,** chopped apples, and raisins.

14 **Add a dab of Dijon mustard** and chopped fresh tarragon.

15 **Elevate the ordinary with a chopped hard-cooked egg** and sweet pickle relish.

15 ways to doctor a deli-roasted chicken

FOR EASY WEEKNIGHT SUPPERS AND HOLIDAY ENTERTAINING, you can't beat the ease of deli-roasted chicken.

1 **Remove the meat from the bones** and fold the chicken into a homemade white sauce or jar of Alfredo sauce. Add sautéed mushrooms, a bit of sherry, and grated Parmesan cheese and spoon this creamed chicken over toast points or corn bread for company or family.

2 **Quarter the chicken** and wrap it in foil with fresh oregano, rosemary, and sliced fresh lemons. Warm in the oven and serve with mashed potatoes.

3 **Quarter the chicken** and place the pieces over stuffing mix to which you have added fresh parsley, celery, and onions. Bake, covered, until warmed through.

4 **Turn the meat into your own chicken salad** to make holiday buffet sandwiches or to stuff in pastry shells.

5 **Make mini chicken and ham sandwiches** with little buttered soft supermarket bakery rolls. Spread on a dab of cranberry sauce.

6 **Glaze the warm chicken with teriyaki sauce** blended with honey. Sprinkle with sesame seeds. Serve with a bright fresh vegetable stir-fry of pea pods, pepper strips, water chestnuts, and green onions. Serve with rice or Asian noodles.

7 **Make a quick but fancy-looking chicken potpie with frozen puff pastry.** Blend chicken with sautéed onions and celery and vegetables of your choice, such as frozen peas, broccoli, or a frozen blend. Mix in two cans of cream of chicken soup and a can of milk. Add a dash of sherry. Bake in a casserole topped with puff pastry strips cut to fit until bubbly and golden brown.

8 **For an easy Moroccan feast,** cook instant couscous with butter, raisins, slivered almonds, canned drained chickpeas, diced zucchini, and diced carrots. Sprinkle warm deli chicken with paprika and cumin. Serve the chicken over the couscous and sprinkle with fresh mint or cilantro.

9 **To your usual fettucine Alfredo,** add shredded chicken, sautéed mushrooms, and fresh spinach leaves that you allow to wilt in the warm sauce.

10 **Warm quarters of the chicken** in the oven along with chunks of kielbasa sausage. Cook a packaged saffron rice mix with sautéed red bell peppers and onions. Top the rice with the warm chicken and sausage and garnish the top with thawed and warmed frozen peas for a fast Spanish paella.

11 **Rub the chicken with coarse-grain mustard** and sprinkle with fresh rosemary. Warm in the oven and serve with mashed potatoes and green beans.

12 **Serve deli chicken with a packaged risotto** doctored up with sautéed sliced fresh mushrooms and a splash of dry white wine.

13 **Deli chicken can be the start of a terrific traditional holiday menu for a small family.** Serve the traditional sides available already prepared in the deli, such as mashed potatoes, dressing, cranberry relish, and green beans. To make the chicken look as grand as a turkey, baste the outside with melted butter blended with a little chicken broth and a pinch of the dried herbs of your choice. Warm loosely covered with foil in the oven.

14 **Deli chicken rubbed with chili powder, garlic powder, and ground cumin** is the centerpiece of a fabulous holiday fiesta. Serve with canned Ranch-style beans sprinkled with queso fresco. Blend a slaw mix with lots of chopped fresh cilantro and a carton of fresh salsa and moisten to taste with mayo and fresh lime juice. Serve warm flour and corn tortillas on the side.

15 **A main-dish winter chicken salad is a nice change of taste.** Arrange deli chicken chunks over peppery watercress, avocado, and orange segments. Top with crumbled feta cheese. Dress with a bottled vinaigrette.

15 ways to doctor deli-boiled shrimp

1 **Fold the prepared shrimp into a creamy pasta sauce.** Add a dash of sherry.

2 **Serve warm or chilled cream soups** from the deli topped with a cooked shrimp for a sophisticated look.

3 **Add deli-cooked shrimp to canned shrimp bisque.** Garnish with lemon slices and parsley or fresh herbs.

4 **Toss deli shrimp with vinaigrette dressing** and a spoonful of pickling spice for a quick pickled shrimp appetizer.

5 **Sauté shrimp with a frozen stir-fry medley** and season with teriyaki sauce. Serve over rice for a quick and healthy supper.

6 **Serve shrimp cocktail with prepared salsa** and fresh avocado as an elegant first course for a holiday supper.

7 **Serve shrimp with a creamy Louis sauce** (mayo blended with chili sauce and sweet pickle relish) on lettuce cups.

8 **Serve a salad of cooked shrimp with sliced avocado,** orange or grapefruit segments, and sliced red onion.

9 **Make a quick Shrimp Newburg with a container of Alfredo sauce.** Flavor with sautéed shallots and sherry. Place in individual gratin dishes, cover with buttered bread crumbs, and broil until bubbly and crisp.

10 **Toss chilled shrimp with pesto** and serve with toothpicks at a cocktail party.

11 **Wrap peeled shrimp in** thin pieces of prosciutto, thread onto skewers, and drizzle with an olive oil and balsamic dressing.

12 **Chop shrimp and blend with Old Bay seasoning** and softened butter and spread on white toast points.

13 **Chop shrimp and blend with salsa and avocado.** Roll in flour tortillas with lettuce leaves. Cut into 1-inch pieces to serve.

14 **Toss shrimp with orange segments,** Kalamata olives, red onion slivers, and strips of fresh fennel. Drizzle with olive oil.

15 **Thread shrimp on skewers** and serve with a bottled Thai peanut dipping sauce.

15 ways to doctor deli pound cake

STORE-BOUGHT POUND CAKE is the beginning of many fantastic holiday desserts.

HOLIDAY TERRINES. Slice the pound cake loaf into thirds horizontally, then layer, chill or freeze, slice, and serve.

1 Candy Cane Terrine: Layer the cake with peppermint ice cream. Drizzle the top with chocolate sauce and crushed candy canes.

2 Ambrosia Terrine: Layer the cake with orange sherbet. Top with an orange glaze made with orange juice and confectioners' sugar. Sprinkle with grated coconut.

3 Amaretto Terrine: Layer the cake with chocolate almond ice cream. Drizzle with a glaze made with Amaretto and confectioners' sugar. Top with chopped toasted almonds.

4 Chocolate Terrine: Moisten layers of cake with your favorite liqueur. Layer the cake with chocolate ice cream. Drizzle with chocolate sauce.

5 Bananas Foster Terrine: Layer sliced bananas and butterscotch pudding laced with Jack Daniel's between pound cake layers. Drizzle the top with bottled caramel sauce and chopped toasted pecans.

POUND CAKE TRIFLES. Pull out your prettiest crystal bowl and layer the cake with all sorts of goodies.

6 English Pound Cake Trifle: Doctor instant vanilla pudding with real vanilla extract and a tablespoon of melted butter. Cut the pound cake into slices and cut each slice into three fingers. Layer a trifle bowl with pound cake fingers sprinkled with cream sherry or Marsala. Spread with a generous layer of raspberry jam. Sprinkle in fresh raspberries, pudding, whipped cream, fruit, and cake. Top with more whipped cream and toasted sliced or slivered almonds.

7 Pound Cake Tiramisù: Cut the pound cake into thin slices and place half of them in the bottom of the serving bowl. Drizzle with strong cold coffee. Top with grated dark chocolate. Top with a layer of sweetened mascarpone cheese blended with sugar and whipped cream and a little Marsala. Top with one more layer of everything, ending with the mascarpone mixture. Top with grated chocolate.

8 Cranberry Pear Trifle: Layer the pound cake fingers with vanilla pudding, canned cranberry relish, and canned pear slices. Top with whipped cream.

9 Mincemeat Trifle: Layer the cake with vanilla pudding flavored with cinnamon, mincemeat from a jar, and whipped cream.

10 Snowball Trifle: Drizzle pound cake fingers with cream of coconut and layer in the trifle bowl with vanilla pudding to which you add whipped cream and shredded coconut. Top with a thick layer of additional shredded coconut.

FANCY POUND CAKE TOPPERS

11 Serve slices of pound cake with whipped cream blended with tangy lemon curd.

12 Toast buttered pound cake slices. Serve with vanilla ice cream, caramel sauce, and toasted pecans.

13 For a Sicilian twist, serve pound cake slices with a dollop of sweetened ricotta cheese blended with rum, whipped cream, and candied fruits.

14 Serve pound cake slices with dried figs soaked in whiskey, creamy mascarpone, and a drizzle of honey.

15 Cut pound cake into thin slices. Spread with cherry jam. Top with another pound cake slice and cut into fingers. Sprinkle with confectioners' sugar and serve these dessert sandwiches on a nice platter.

15 ways to doctor deli cheeses

1 Alternate slices of fresh mozzarella with sliced tomatoes and fresh basil leaves on a pretty plate. Drizzle with olive oil and sprinkle with a little salt.

2 Toss hot spaghetti with fresh mozzarella cubes, chopped tomatoes, pressed garlic, salt, and fresh basil.

3 Combine shredded Swiss cheese, a little minced onion, and enough mayonnaise to pull this together. Pile onto sturdy bread and run under the broiler until bubbly. Cut into squares and serve as a quick appetizer.

4 Make huevos rancheros. Warm your favorite salsa, fry some eggs, and shred Monterey Jack cheese. Place a lightly fried corn tortilla on each plate; top with a fried egg, warm salsa, and shredded cheese. Garnish with cilantro.

5 Sandwich slices of pepper Jack cheese between sourdough bread along with a slice of tomato and slice of crisp bacon. Brush with olive oil and cook on a griddle on both sides until crispy.

6 Layer slices of cheese and sandwich meats onto a flour tortilla, then slather with an herbed mayonnaise or favorite salad dressing. Top with shredded lettuce or carrots, then roll up, and slice into bite-size pieces.

7 Chop sliced Swiss cheese and ham and place on top of a mixed green salad along with half of a hard-cooked egg for a satisfying chef's salad supper.

8 Cut a small round of Camembert into 1-inch pieces and toss with hot cooked potato cubes, oil, and vinegar for a warm potato salad.

9 Encase a small round of Camembert in puff pastry dough, brush with a beaten egg, and bake at 375°F until the pastry has browned all over.

10 Melt American cheese over low heat and add canned tomatoes and chiles. Stir and cook until well combined. Serve with tortilla chips as a speedy appetizer. Keep this chili con queso warm in a slow cooker.

11 **Shred any combination of deli cheese** and store in a plastic bag. By the handful, add this as a filling for omelets.

12 **Cut a long loaf of French bread in half horizontally.** Brush the split sides with garlic butter, then pile on shredded Cheddar or Colby cheese. Run under the broiler until the cheese bubbles, then slice and serve.

13 **Bake large Idaho potatoes until tender.** When they are cool enough to handle, cut off the top third, and scoop out the cooked potato into a bowl. Season with milk, butter, and salt and pepper to taste. Pack this mixture back into the potato, pack with shredded deli cheese such as Cheddar or Colby, then bake at 350°F until the twice-baked potatoes are cooked through and the cheese has melted.

Use my doctoring techniques to turn supermarket convenience foods into dishes that taste so good you will think they're made totally from scratch.

14 **Slice ripe tomatoes in half crosswise** and squeeze to remove juice. Scoop out the pulp and mash with a little feta cheese, chopped onion, salt, and pepper. Pack back into the tomatoes and top with bread crumbs and a drizzle of olive oil. Broil until golden.

15 **Nothing is more festive than fondue.** Rub a heatproof casserole with garlic, pour in a cup of white wine, and add a pound of shredded Gruyère, a bit at a time, stirring with a wooden spoon while over low heat. Season with pepper, salt; nutmeg and serve with long forks and French bread cubes.

15 ways to doctor deli hors d'oeuvres

NOWADAYS YOU CAN PUT TOGETHER AN AMAZING SELECTION OF APPETIZERS WITHOUT COOKING. Choose wisely and creatively from the offerings in the supermarket.

1 **Hummus comes in a variety of flavors.** Serve a few different flavors in small bowls surrounded by pita chips and fresh veggies. Garnish each with an ingredient in that flavor so guests know what they are, such as a Kalamata olive on top for the black olive hummus or chopped red pepper for the red pepper hummus.

2 **Top plain hummus** with Christmas red pomegranate seeds.

3 **Serve hummus on a large flat plate** surrounded by pita chips stuck into the dip like a wreath.

4 **Spread prepared spinach dip or artichoke dip** on toasted thinly sliced French bread and place under the broiler until bubbly. Top these bruschetta with sliced almonds or roasted red pepper strips.

5 **Make a quick antipasti platter** with a variety of Italian deli meats, such as cappocolla, sopressata, and salami. Get the deli to slice them paper thin and casually mound them on a platter with deli marinated mozzarella and a variety of deli olives; or roll them around lightly steamed asparagus spears.

6 **Wrap one end of long bread sticks** with paper-thin slices of prosciutto or salami. Lay the sticks on a platter with olives.

7 **Pick a variety of already washed and sliced colorful bell peppers** and other specialty veggies at the salad bar. Pick up a colorful deli dip to go with them.

8 **Slice a deli fresh pineapple into chunks** and scatter with pomegranate seeds. Serve with frilly toothpicks.

9 **What could be easier or more sophisticated** than a big, beautiful hunk of Stilton cheese on a platter with grapes and a scattering of toasted walnut halves?

10 **Pacific smoked salmon** needs nothing more than capers, onions, chopped hard-cooked egg, and crackers alongside. Or blend some smoked salmon into deli egg salad for a quick spread.

11 **Here are some easy blend-ins for egg salad** that turn this simple mixture into a great holiday spread for melba toast and crackers: caviar, almonds, fresh herbs, olives, salmon, and roasted red pepper bits.

12 **Place a single layer of cherry or grape tomatoes** with toothpicks in a shallow pool of vodka or tequila. Set a dipping bowl of seasoned salt or kosher salt to the side for dipping.

13 **Top a small round of Brie cheese with cranberry chutney.** Blend some cranberry sauce with a jar of chutney or simply add dried cranberries to the chutney.

14 **Make deli tortellini** salad seem more like an appetizer by serving it with picks. Serve in a flat bowl blended with deli marinated mushroom caps. Add freshness with parsley or other herbs.

15 **Any deli salad** (chicken, tuna, egg, etc.) served in prepared mini pastry shells is suddenly an appetizer. Decorate the tops with chopped parsley or snipped chives.

fast & fabulous finales

Check out these quick fixes for spectacular holiday desserts.

Chocolate Fantasies

Indulge a chocolate-lover's dream with these dark and decadent desserts.

Warm Chocolate Cupcakes with Molten Centers

MAKES: 22 to 24 cupcakes (2½ inches each)
PREPARATION TIME: 25 minutes
BAKING TIME: 10 to 11 minutes

Basic Chocolate Ganache, chilled at least 1 hour
Cinnamon Crème Anglaise
Vegetable oil cooking spray, for misting the pans
Unsweetened cocoa powder, for dusting the pans
1 package (18.25 ounces) plain devil's food cake mix
1 cup water
½ cup vegetable oil
3 large eggs
1 teaspoon pure vanilla extract
½ teaspoon ground cinnamon
¼ cup confectioners' sugar, for dusting cupcakes

PREPARE the Basic Chocolate Ganache, cover it with plastic wrap, and place it in the refrigerator to chill. Prepare the Cinnamon Crème Anglaise, cover it with plastic wrap placed right on the surface, and place it in the refrigerator to chill.

PLACE a rack in the center of the oven and preheat the oven to 400°F. Lightly mist 24 cupcake cups with vegetable oil cooking spray and dust them with cocoa. Shake out the excess cocoa. Set the pans aside.

PLACE the cake mix, water, oil, eggs, vanilla, and cinnamon in a large mixing bowl. Blend with an electric mixer on low speed for 30 seconds. Stop the machine and scrape down the sides of the bowl with a rubber spatula. Increase the mixer speed to medium and blend 1½ to 2 minutes more, scraping down the sides again if needed. The batter should look well combined and thickened. Spoon or scoop ⅓ cup batter into each prepared cup, filling it two-thirds full. Drop a heaping teaspoonful of ganache onto the top of the batter in each cup. Place the pans in the oven.

BAKE the cupcakes until the cake bakes up around the ganache, the tops are domed, and the cupcakes spring back when lightly pressed with your finger, 10 to 11 minutes. Remove the pans from the oven and place them on wire racks for 1 minute. Run a dinner knife around the edges of the cupcake cups, lift the cupcakes up from the bottoms of the cups using the end of the knife, and pick them out of the cups carefully with your fingertips. Place them on dessert plates, sift confectioners' sugar over the top, spoon the Cinnamon Crème Anglaise in a pool around each cupcake, and serve warm.

NOTE: Store these cupcakes, in a cake saver or under a glass dome, at room temperature for up to 1 day. To reheat so the centers are molten once again, place the cupcakes on a microwave-safe plate and cover with paper towels. Heat on high power for 10 seconds, carefully remove, and serve.

Basic Chocolate Ganache

MAKES: 2 cups
PREPARATION TIME: 5 minutes
CHILL TIME: 1 hour

¾ cup heavy (whipping) cream
1⅓ cups semisweet chocolate chips
1 tablespoon liqueur of your choice or 1 teaspoon pure vanilla extract (optional)

PLACE the cream in a small heavy saucepan over medium heat. Bring it to a boil, stirring. Meanwhile, place the chocolate chips in a large stainless steel mixing bowl. Remove the cream from the heat and pour it over the chocolate. Stir with a wooden spoon until the chocolate has melted. Stir in the liqueur if desired. Let chill for 1 hour so it thickens into a spreadable consistency.

Cinnamon Crème Anglaise

MAKES: 2 cups
PREPARATION TIME: 5 minutes
COOKING TIME: 15 to 17 minutes

2 cups milk
5 tablespoons sugar
Pinch of salt
4 large egg yolks
1 teaspoon pure vanilla extract
½ teaspoon ground cinnamon

PLACE the milk, sugar, and salt in a heavy-bottomed medium-size saucepan over medium-high heat. Cook, stirring with a wooden spoon, until the sugar dissolves, 2 to 3 minutes.

MEANWHILE, place the egg yolks in a medium-size mixing bowl and beat with a fork until lemon-colored. Remove the saucepan from the heat and ladle a large spoonful of the hot milk mixture over the egg yolks, stirring the yolks gently. Transfer the yolks to the milk mixture and stir to combine. Place the pan over medium-low heat and cook, stirring constantly, until the sauce thickens, 13 to 14 minutes. Remove the pan from the heat and stir in the vanilla and cinnamon.

SPOON a generous tablespoonful of the warm sauce onto plates and place cupcakes on it. Or chill the sauce and serve cold alongside the cupcakes.

Mocha Brownie Cheesecake

SERVES: 20
PREPARATION TIME: 15 minutes
BAKING TIME: 45 to 50 minutes
CHILL TIME: 1 hour

1 package (18.25 ounces) plain devil's food cake mix
6 tablespoons (¾ stick) butter, melted
1 large egg
½ teaspoon ground cinnamon
2 cups semisweet chocolate chips
2 packages (8 ounces each) cream cheese, at room temperature
1 can (14 ounces) sweetened condensed milk

just combined, 30 seconds. Stop the machine, add the 3 eggs and the yogurt, and beat on medium speed for 1 minute. Stop the machine and scrape down the sides of the bowl with the rubber spatula. Pour the filling onto the crust and spread it out with the rubber spatula so that it covers the entire surface and reaches the sides of the pan. Place the pan in the oven.

BAKE the cheesecake until it looks shiny and the center jiggles only slightly when you shake the pan, 45 to 50 minutes (it will firm up after cooling). Remove the pan from the oven and place it on a wire rack to cool for 30 minutes. Then lightly cover the pan with plastic wrap and place it in the refrigerator to chill for at least 1 hour, or preferably 24 hours, for the flavors to meld.

MEANWHILE, prepare the Sweetened Cream.

CUT cheesecake into squares and serve with a dollop of Sweetened Cream and a sprinkling of cinnamon, instant coffee powder, or grated chocolate if desired.

NOTE: Store this cake, covered first in plastic wrap and then in aluminum foil, in the refrigerator for up to 1 week. Or freeze it, wrapped in foil, for up to 2 months; thaw the cake overnight in the refrigerator before serving.

Sweetened Cream

MAKES: 2 cups
PREPARATION TIME: 4 minutes

1 cup heavy (whipping) cream
¼ cup confectioners' sugar, sifted, or to taste
½ teaspoon pure vanilla extract or pure almond extract

CHILL a large, clean mixing bowl and electric mixer beaters in the freezer for a few minutes while you assemble the ingredients.

POUR the cream into the chilled bowl and beat with the electric mixer on high speed until it thickens, 1½ minutes. Stop the machine and add the confectioners' sugar and the vanilla extract. Beat the cream on high speed until stiff peaks form, 1 to 2 minutes more.

Warm Chocolate Cupcakes with Molten Centers

3 large eggs
½ cup coffee or vanilla fat-free yogurt
1 cup Sweetened Cream or frozen whipped topping, thawed
Ground cinnamon, instant coffee powder, or grated chocolate, for garnish (optional)

PLACE a rack in the center of the oven and preheat the oven to 325°F. Set aside a 13- by 9-inch pan.

PLACE the cake mix, melted butter, 1 egg, and cinnamon in a large mixing bowl. Blend with an electric mixer on low speed for 2 minutes. Stop the machine and scrape down the sides of the bowl with a rubber spatula. The batter should come together into a ball. With your fingertips, pat the batter evenly over the bottom and 1 inch up the sides of the pan, spreading it out with your fingers until smooth. Set the pan aside.

MELT the chocolate chips in a medium-size glass bowl in the microwave oven on high power for 1½ minutes. Remove the bowl from the oven and stir with a small rubber spatula until the chocolate is melted. Allow it to cool slightly.

PLACE the melted chocolate, cream cheese, and sweetened condensed milk in the same mixing bowl that was used for the crust. With the same beaters (no need to clean them either), blend with an electric mixer on low speed until

Quick Tunnel-of-Fudge Cake

SERVES: 16
PREPARATION TIME: 12 minutes
BAKING TIME: 45 to 50 minutes

1½ cups milk
1 package (3.4 ounces) chocolate
    fudge pudding and pie filling mix
    (not instant)
1 cup semisweet chocolate chips
1 tablespoon butter
Vegetable oil cooking spray, for
    misting the pan
Flour, for dusting the pan
1 package (18.25 ounces) devil's food
    cake mix with pudding
½ cup vegetable oil
½ cup sour cream
½ cup water

4 large eggs
1 teaspoon pure vanilla extract
2 cups finely chopped walnuts
Martha's Chocolate Icing

PLACE the milk in a medium-size saucepan and whisk in the pudding mix. Cook, stirring, over medium heat until the mixture comes to a boil, 4 to 5 minutes. Remove the pan from the heat and stir in the chocolate chips and butter. Stir until the pudding is smooth and thickened and the chocolate has melted. Set the pan aside.

PLACE a rack in the center of the oven and preheat the oven to 350°F. Lightly mist a 12-cup Bundt pan with vegetable oil cooking spray, then dust with flour. Shake out the excess flour. Set the pan aside. Place the cake mix, oil, sour cream, water, eggs, and vanilla in a large mixing bowl. Blend with an electric mixer on low speed for 1 minute. Stop the machine and scrape down the sides of the bowl with a rubber spatula. Increase the mixer speed to medium and beat 2 minutes more, scraping down the sides again if needed. The batter should look thick and well combined. Fold in the walnuts, making sure they are well distributed throughout the batter.

RESERVE 2 cups of the batter. Pour the remaining batter into the prepared pan. Spoon the pudding filling in a ring on top of the batter, making sure it does not touch the sides of the pan. Spoon the reserved batter over the filling, smoothing it out with the rubber spatula. Place the pan in the oven.

BAKE the cake until it springs back when lightly pressed with your finger and is just starting to pull away from the sides of the pan, 45 to 50 minutes. Remove the pan from the oven and place it on a wire rack to cool for 20 minutes. Run a long, sharp knife around the edge of the cake and invert it onto a rack to cool completely, 20 minutes more.

MEANWHILE, prepare Martha's Chocolate Icing.

PLACE the cake on a serving platter and pour the warm icing over it. Let the cake rest for 10 minutes before slicing. Slice and serve.

NOTE: Store this cake, wrapped in aluminum foil or plastic wrap, or in a cake saver, at room temperature for up to 1 week. Or freeze it, wrapped in foil, for up to 6 months; thaw the cake overnight in the refrigerator before serving.

Martha's Chocolate Icing
MAKES: 1½ cups
PREPARATION TIME: 8 minutes

1 cup sugar
5 tablespoons butter
⅓ cup milk
1 cup semisweet chocolate chips

PLACE the sugar, butter, and milk in a medium-size saucepan over medium-high heat. Stir until the mixture comes to a boil, 3 to 4 minutes. Still stirring, let the mixture boil until the sugar dissolves, 1 minute. Remove the pan from the heat.

---

15 ways to doctor a brownie mix

BROWNIE MIXES are an easy part of our everyday dessert repertoire. They are particularly useful during the holidays when you need to entertain a crowd or bring a dish to a party. Here is how you can turn the ordinary into the extraordinary.

1 **Fold white chocolate chunks** and macadamia nuts into the batter before baking.

2 **Stir chopped candy canes** and white chocolate chunks into the batter.

3 **Sprinkle red and green M&Ms** on top of the batter just before baking.

4 **Add a dash of peppermint extract** to the batter and fold in a cup of mint chocolate chips.

5 **Fold in chopped peppermint patties** just before baking.

6 **Chill Reese's Peanut Butter Cups and chop them coarsely.** Fold them into the batter before baking.

7 **Add a couple of tablespoons of strong brewed coffee** to the batter.

8 **For dinner parties,** turn brownies into an easy dessert. Top with pink peppermint ice cream and drizzle with chocolate sauce. Or top with vanilla ice cream and crushed candy canes, then top with chocolate sauce. Or top with vanilla ice cream, caramel sauce, and toasted pecans.

9 **For a more adult version,** top a brownie with a scoop of vanilla or coffee ice cream, then drizzle with the liqueur of your choice—coffee, peppermint, hazelnut, almond, or orange.

10 **Make German chocolate cake frosting** with coconut and pecans and spread it on brownies after they cool.

11 **Fold a cup of toffee bar bits** and a cup of butterscotch chips into the batter before baking.

12 **Stir cinnamon into the batter** for a Mexican-style brownie.

13 **Don't forget this old trick:** Make a snowflake pattern on the top of brownies by sifting powdered sugar over snowflake shapes from doilies.

14 **Cut brownies into interesting shapes:** triangles, rectangle fingers, or circles.

15 **Under-bake a batch of brownies.** Cut them into squares after they cool, then form into balls. Roll these brownie balls into sweetened cocoa powder or finely chopped nuts just like truffles.

STIR in the chocolate chips and continue to stir until the mixture is smooth and the chocolate has melted.

Chocolate-Almond Fudge Torte

SERVES: 16
PREPARATION TIME: 43 minutes
COOKING TIME: 25 to 27 minutes
RESTING TIME: 1 hour, 5 minutes

¼ cup semisweet chocolate chips
12 maraschino cherries with stems, for garnish (optional)
Vegetable oil cooking spray, for misting the pans
Unsweetened cocoa powder, for dusting the pans
1 package (18.25 ounces) plain devil's food cake mix
1 package (3.4 ounces) vanilla instant pudding mix
3 large eggs
1¼ cups milk
1 cup vegetable oil
¾ teaspoon almond extract
Chocolate Ganache
2 milk chocolate bars (1.55 ounces each), cut diagonally into shards
1 cup sliced almonds, toasted
Additional chocolate shards and toasted almonds, for garnish (optional)

PLACE chocolate chips in a small custard cup. Microwave at high power for 30 seconds. Stir until the chocolate is smooth. Dip the cherries about half way into the melted chocolate, placing them on a waxed paper-lined plate. Place the chocolate-dipped cherries in the refrigerator while preparing the cake.

PLACE a rack in the center of the oven and preheat the oven to 350°. Mist two 9-inch cake pans with vegetable oil cooking spray, then dust with cocoa. Shake out the excess cocoa and set the pans aside.

COMBINE the cake mix, pudding mix, eggs, milk, oil, and almond extract in a large bowl. Blend with an electric mixer on low speed 1 minute. Stop the machine and scrape down the sides of the bowl with a rubber spatula. Beat 2 minutes more at medium speed, scraping down the sides again if needed. The

Chocolate-Almond Fudge Torte

batter should look blended and smooth. Divide the batter evenly among the prepared pans, smoothing it out with the rubber spatula. Place the pans in the oven.

BAKE the cakes until they spring back when lightly touched in the center, 25 to 27 minutes.

REMOVE the pans from the oven and place them on wire racks to cool for 10 minutes. Run a dinner knife around the edge of each layer and invert each on a rack, then invert them again onto another rack so that the cakes are right side up. Cool completely.

MEANWHILE, prepare the Chocolate Ganache.

SPLIT the cooled cake layers in half horizontally to make four layers. Place ¾ cup of Chocolate Ganache in a small glass bowl and set aside.

PLACE one cake layer, cut side up, on a serving platter. Spread the top with 1 cup of ganache, then top with one-third of the chocolate shards and ⅓ cup of the almonds. Top with another cake layer. Repeat the procedure twice, ending with a cake layer. Spread the remaining ganache on the sides and the top of the cake. Place the cake in the refrigerator to chill.

MEANWHILE, heat reserved ¾ cup ganache in the microwave on high power for 15 seconds, then stir until smooth. Chill the ganache for 10 minutes or just

until thickened, but still pourable. Remove the cake from the refrigerator and pour the ganache in the center of the cake, letting excess run over the edges. Arrange 6 chocolate-covered cherries and, if desired, additional chocolate shards and toasted almonds in the center of the cake. Arrange remaining cherries at the sides of the cake. Chill cake thoroughly before serving.

NOTE: Store this cake, in a cake saver, in the refrigerator for up to 1 week.

Chocolate Ganache

MAKES: 5¾ cups
PREPARATION TIME: 2 minutes
COOKING TIME: 3 minutes
RESTING TIME: 45 minutes

5⅓ cups semisweet chocolate chips (2 pounds)
1½ cups heavy (whipping) cream
2 tablespoons Amaretto

PLACE the chocolate chips and cream in a medium-size glass bowl. Microwave at high power for 2 minutes, then stir and microwave 1 minute more at high power. Stir until smooth, then stir in the Amaretto. Transfer the ganache to a metal bowl and allow to cool until spreading consistency, about 45 minutes, stirring occasionally.

Cupcake Christmas Tree

Cupcake Tree

Let scrumptious desserts do double duty as the table centerpiece
with a sensational holiday cake baked in single servings.

Cupcake Christmas Tree

SERVES: up to 16
PREPARATION TIME: 10 minutes

Cream Cheese Frosting
Green food coloring paste
12 or 16 cupcakes of your choice,
    baked in paper liners
Chocolate sprinkles
18- by 12-inch platter or board
Colorful candies, such as gumdrops,
    M&M's, or Skittles
Popcorn strings, for garnish (optional)

PREPARE the Cream Cheese Frosting. Once it is sufficiently beaten, set aside about 2 heaping tablespoonfuls. Tint the rest with ½ teaspoon of the green food coloring.
PLACE 1 heaping tablespoon of the untinted frosting on each of the two cupcakes and swirl to spread it out with a short metal spatula or a spoon, taking care to cover the tops completely. Cover the untinted frosting heavily with the chocolate sprinkles. Frost the remaining cupcakes with the tinted frosting. Set the cupcakes aside.
SET the platter on a work surface with the short side closest to you. Place one cupcake near the top of the platter. Place two cupcakes side by side below it. Place three cupcakes side by side below the row of two cupcakes. Place four cupcakes side by side below the row of three. And place four more cupcakes side by side below the row of four if needed. Make sure the rows form a neat triangular Christmas tree shape. For the trunk, place the two cupcakes with chocolate sprinkles in the center below the four cupcakes.
DECORATE the green-tinted cupcakes with the colorful candies to resemble ornaments. Garnish with popcorn strings if desired.

NOTE: If not serving the cupcake tree immediately, wait to put on the candies and popcorn strings. Refrigerate undecorated tree lightly covered with waxed paper or plastic wrap for up to 3 days. Decorate with the candies and popcorn right before serving.

Cream Cheese Frosting

MAKES: 3 cups
PREPARATION TIME: 5 minutes

1 package (8 ounces) reduced-fat
    cream cheese, at room temperature
4 tablespoons (½ stick) butter, at
    room temperature
6 cups sifted confectioners' sugar
2 teaspoons pure vanilla extract

PLACE the cream cheese and butter in a large mixing bowl. Blend with an electric mixer on low speed until combined, 30 seconds for either batch. Stop the machine. Add the confectioners' sugar, a little at a time, blending with the mixer on low speed until the sugar is well incorporated, 1 minute. Add the vanilla, then increase the mixer speed to medium and blend the frosting until fluffy, 1 minute more.

Little Chocolate Bar Cakes

MAKES: 1 dozen
PREPARATION TIME: 20 minutes
FREEZING TIME: at least 3 hours,
    preferably overnight
ASSEMBLY TIME: 5 minutes

12 foil liners for cupcake pans
    (2½-inch size)
¾ cup graham cracker crumbs
¼ cup finely chopped almonds
3 tablespoons butter, melted
6 small bars (1.45 ounces each)
    Hershey's Milk Chocolate with
    Almonds
3½ cups miniature marshmallows
    (half a 10.5-ounce bag)
½ cup milk
1 cup heavy (whipping) cream
2 to 3 tablespoons toasted almonds,
    for garnish (optional)

2 tablespoons grated semisweet
    chocolate, for garnish (optional)

LINE 12 cupcake cups with the foil liners and set the pan aside.
PREPARE the crusts. Place the cracker crumbs, almonds, and melted butter in a mixing bowl and stir to combine. Spoon about 1 tablespoon of the mixture into each liner, pressing down with your fingers to make the crust.
PREPARE the filling. Break up the Hershey bars and place them in a large saucepan over low heat with the marshmallows and milk. Heat, stirring frequently with a wooden spoon, until the chocolate and marshmallows melt and the mixture thickens, 10 minutes. Remove the pan from the heat and let the mixture cool slightly, 5 minutes.
PLACE the electric mixer beaters and a large mixing bowl in the freezer for 1 minute. Remove both, pour the cream into the chilled bowl, and beat with the electric mixer on high speed until stiff peaks form, 2 to 3 minutes.
FOLD 1 cup of the whipped cream into the chocolate mixture until well combined. Place the remaining whipped cream, covered, in the refrigerator. Top the crusts with the chocolate mixture, dividing it evenly among them. The liners should be very full but not overflowing. Cover the pan with plastic wrap and place it in the freezer until firm, at least 3 hours.
REMOVE the cupcake pan from the freezer 15 minutes before serving. To serve, place a dinner knife underneath the liners and lift out the cakes. Peel away the liners and place the cupcakes on serving plates. Dollop the top of the cupcakes with 1 heaping tablespoon of the reserved whipped cream and garnish with toasted almonds and grated chocolate. The cakes are ready to serve.

NOTE: Freeze these "cupcakes," covered with plastic wrap, for up to 2 weeks.

Holiday Gift Cupcakes

Holiday Gift Cupcakes

MAKES: 22 to 24 cupcakes
PREPARATION TIME: 10 minutes
BAKING TIME: 18 to 20 minutes

24 silver or gold foil liners for cupcake
    pans (2½-inch size)
1 package (18.25 ounces) German
    chocolate cake mix with pudding
1 cup sour cream
½ cup water
¼ cup vegetable oil
3 large eggs
1 bottle (1 ounce) red liquid food
    coloring
1 teaspoon pure vanilla extract
Cream Cheese Frosting
Red liquid or paste food coloring
Red sugar sprinkles (optional)
24 Meringue Bows and Ribbons

PLACE a rack in the center of the oven and preheat the oven to 350°F. Line 24 cupcake cups with foil liners. Set the pans aside.

PREPARE the cupcake batter. Place the cake mix, sour cream, water, oil, eggs, bottle of food coloring, and vanilla extract in a large mixing bowl. Blend with an electric mixer on low speed for 30 seconds. Stop the machine and scrape down the sides of the bowl with a rubber spatula. Increase the mixer speed to medium and beat 2 minutes more, scraping down the sides again if needed. Spoon or scoop ⅓ cup batter into each lined cupcake cup, filling it two-thirds full. (You will get between 22 and 24 cupcakes; remove the empty liners, if any.) Place the pans in the oven.

BAKE the cupcakes until they spring back when lightly pressed with your finger, 18 to 20 minutes. Remove the pans from the oven and place them on wire racks to cool for 5 minutes. Run a dinner knife around the edges of the cupcake liners, lift the cupcakes up from the bottoms of the cups using the end of the knife, and pick them out of the cups carefully with your fingertips. Place them on a wire rack to cool for 15 minutes before frosting.

MEANWHILE, prepare the Cream Cheese Frosting, adding additional red food coloring once the frosting is sufficiently beaten. Start with 3 drops and blend them in well. If the color isn't red enough, keep adding more color 1 drop at a time until the frosting is a deep red all over (or to your liking).

PLACE 1 heaping tablespoon of frosting on each cupcake and swirl to spread it out with a short metal spatula or a spoon, taking care to cover the tops completely. Sprinkle the red sugar sprinkles over the top if desired.

REMOVE the meringue bows from the waxed paper, by pushing the bows carefully from underneath the waxed paper to loosen. Sit a bow straight up on each cupcake and place two

When everyone is eager to open a gift on Christmas Eve, these festive cupcakes with their pretty bows just might make the waiting a little easier.

meringue ribbons coming from the center of the bow to resemble a gift-wrapped present.

NOTE: Store these cupcakes covered with plastic wrap or in a cake saver without their bows and ribbons, in the refrigerator for up to 3 days. Add the bows and ribbons just before serving.

Cream Cheese Frosting
MAKES: 4 cups
PREPARATION TIME: 5 minutes

1 package (8 ounces) reduced-fat cream cheese, at room temperature
4 tablespoons (½ stick) butter, at room temperature
6 cups sifted confectioners' sugar
2 teaspoons pure vanilla extract

PLACE the cream cheese and butter in a large mixing bowl. Blend with an electric mixer on low speed until combined, 30 seconds. Stop the machine. Add the confectioners' sugar, a little at a time, blending with the mixer on low speed until the sugar is well incorporated, 1 minute. Add the vanilla, then increase the mixer speed to medium and blend the frosting until fluffy, 1 minute more.

Meringue Bows and Ribbons
PREPARATION TIME: 20 minutes
ASSEMBLY TIME: 20 minutes

4 cups confectioners' sugar
3 tablespoons powdered egg whites
6 tablespoons water, plus more for thinning
White, gold, or silver edible glitter

AT least 3 hours before baking the cupcakes, prepare the meringue bows and ribbons: Line two baking sheets with waxed paper and set them aside. Place the confectioners' sugar, powdered egg whites, and 6 tablespoons of the water

in a medium-size mixing bowl and beat with an electric mixer until the mixture is stiff, about 2 minutes.

SPOON 1 cup of the egg white mixture into a pastry bag with a #3 or #4 plain round tip. Draw outlines of 24 bows in a fancy figure eight, by slowly piping the mixture onto the waxed paper in the desired bow shape. Now pipe the notched ribbon ends that hang off a tied bow separately. Each bow gets two ribbon ends. Each bow should measure about 2½ inches wide; each ribbon end about 1½ inches long. Leave 2 inches between bows. To prepare the filling for the bows and ribbon pieces, thin the remaining egg white mixture with water until it has the consistency of white school glue. Use either a toothpick or a small plastic knife to fill in the bow and ribbon outlines with the thinned mixture, taking care to fill the corners. While the icing is still wet, sprinkle white, gold, and silver edible glitter on each bow. Allow the meringue bows to dry for at least 3 hours before using.

Mini Strawberry Trifles

MAKES: 8 trifles
PREPARATION TIME: 20 minutes
ASSEMBLY TIME: 2 to 3 minutes

1 package (3.4 ounces) instant vanilla pudding mix
2 cups cold milk
1 teaspoon pure vanilla extract
½ cup heavy (whipping) cream
2 teaspoons confectioners' sugar
8 foil liners for cupcake pans (2½-inch size)
1 small (10.75 ounces) loaf frozen pound cake
2 tablespoons cream sherry
½ cup chopped fresh ripe strawberries
8 whole medium-size ripe strawberries, for garnish (optional)

PREPARE the instant pudding according to the package directions, adding the cold milk as directed. Stir in the vanilla. Immediately place the pudding in the refrigerator to chill until it is needed.

MEANWHILE, place a clean, medium-size mixing bowl and electric mixer beaters in the freezer for 1 minute. Pour the cream into the chilled bowl and beat with the electric mixer on high speed until the cream has thickened, 1½ minutes. Stop the machine and add the sugar. Beat the cream and sugar on high speed until stiff peaks form, 1 to 2 minutes more. Place the whipped cream in the refrigerator to chill.

PLACE the foil liners on a serving platter and set aside.

PLACE the frozen cake on a cutting board. Slice the cake thinly into 16 slices that are about ¼-inch thick. Cut a 2-inch round out of each slice, yielding 16 rounds. Generously brush one side of each round with the sherry.

PLACE 8 rounds, sherry sides up, in the foil liners. Dollop 1 tablespoon of pudding on the top of each cake round. Place 1 tablespoon of chopped strawberries on top of the pudding. Then dollop with 1 tablespoon more of the pudding. Place the remaining eight cake rounds on the top of pudding, sherry sides down. Cover the platter with plastic wrap and chill the cakes until time to serve.

JUST before serving, slice the whole strawberries. Top each trifle with a heaping tablespoonful of whipped cream and garnish with 2 or 3 of the nicest strawberry slices.

NOTE: Store these "cupcakes," covered in plastic wrap or in a cake saver, in the refrigerator for up to 3 days.

Frosty Fixings

Doctored cake mixes make luscious desserts that taste like they're made from scratch.

Italian Cream Cake

SERVES: 12
PREPARATION TIME: 30 minutes
BAKING TIME: 20 minutes
RESTING TIME: 10 minutes

Solid vegetable shortening, for greasing the pans
Flour, for dusting the pans
3 large eggs, separated, plus 2 large egg whites
½ teaspoon cream of tartar
1 package (18.25 ounces) plain white cake mix
1 cup buttermilk
½ cup vegetable oil
1 teaspoon pure vanilla extract
1 cup sweetened flaked coconut

anne's tip

FREEZING UNFROSTED CAKES

With time being your most precious commodity, it makes sense to bake cakes ahead and freeze them for later consumption. And one of the best ways to do this and still allow for that last-minute spontaneity is to bake and freeze unfrosted layers. To prepare unfrosted cakes for freezing, first make sure they have cooled completely on the kitchen counter. Then wrap them well in heavy-duty aluminum foil and place them in a large zipper-lock freezer bag and seal. Or if you don't have any bags, wrap the layers twice in heavy-duty aluminum foil. Place in the coldest part of your freezer—in the back or in the bottom— where they will keep for up to 2 months.

To thaw for frosting, remove the layers from the plastic bag and unwrap the foil at the top so the layers can breathe as they thaw on the counter. This allows the moisture to escape so the cake won't get soggy. When completely thawed, frost the layers and serve.

1 cup finely chopped pecans
1 package (8 ounces) cream cheese, at room temperature
8 tablespoons (1 stick) butter, at room temperature
4 cups confectioners' sugar, sifted
½ teaspoon coconut flavoring
Additional sweetened flaked coconut

PLACE a rack in the center of the oven and preheat the oven to 350°F.

LIGHTLY grease three 9-inch round cake pans with vegetable shortening, then dust them with flour. Shake out the excess flour. Set the pans aside.

PLACE the 5 egg whites and the cream of tartar in a medium-size mixing bowl. Beat with an electric mixer on high speed until stiff peaks form, 2 to 3 minutes. Set the egg whites aside.

PLACE the cake mix, 3 egg yolks, buttermilk, oil, and vanilla in a large mixing bowl and beat on low speed until blended, 1 minute. Stop the machine and scrape down the sides of the bowl with a rubber spatula. Increase the mixer speed to medium and beat for 2 minutes longer, scraping down the sides again if needed. The batter should be well blended. Spoon the beaten egg whites onto the cake batter and, using a rubber spatula, fold them into the batter until the mixture is light but well blended. Gently fold in the coconut and pecans. Divide the batter evenly among the prepared pans, smoothing it out with a rubber spatula. Place the pans in the oven side by side or, if your oven is not large enough, place two pans on the center rack and the third pan in the center of the highest rack.

BAKE the cakes until they spring back when lightly pressed with a finger, 20 minutes. Check the pan on the highest rack first, as it will bake the quickest and may need to be rotated to a lower rack while it bakes.

REMOVE the cakes from the oven and place them on wire racks to cool for 10 minutes. Run a dinner knife around the edge of each layer and invert each cake

onto a rack, then invert them again onto another rack, so that the cakes are right side up. Allow the cakes to cool completely, 15 minutes more.

MEANWHILE, prepare the frosting. Place the cream cheese and butter in a large mixing bowl and beat with an electric mixer on low speed until creamy, 30 seconds. Add the confectioners' sugar and coconut flavoring and beat on low speed until the sugar is incorporated. Increase the mixer speed to high and beat until the frosting is fluffy, 1 minute longer.

TO assemble the cake, place one cake layer, right side up, on a serving plate and spread some of the frosting over the top. Place a second layer, right side up, on top of the first. Spread some of the frosting over the top. Place the third layer, right side up, on top of the second, then frost the top and side generously. Sprinkle with additional coconut.

NOTE: Store this cake, in a cake saver or under a glass dome, in the refrigerator for up to 1 week. Or freeze it, in a cake saver, for up to 6 months; thaw the cake overnight in the refrigerator before serving.

Caramel Cake

SERVES: 16
PREPARATION TIME: 5 to 7 minutes
BAKING TIME: 27 to 29 minutes
ASSEMBLY TIME: 20 minutes

Solid vegetable shortening, for greasing the pans
Flour, for dusting the pans
1 package (18.25 ounces) plain white cake mix
1 cup milk
8 tablespoons (1 stick) butter, melted
3 large eggs
2 teaspoons pure vanilla extract
Quick Caramel Frosting

PLACE a rack in the center of the oven and preheat the oven to 350°F.

Italian Cream Cake

Generously grease two 9-inch round cake pans with solid vegetable shortening, then dust with flour. Shake out the excess flour. Set the pans aside.

PLACE the cake mix, milk, melted butter, eggs, and vanilla extract in a large mixing bowl. Blend with an electric mixer on low speed for 1 minute. Stop the machine and scrape the sides down of the bowl with a rubber spatula. Increase the mixer speed to medium and beat 2 minutes more, scraping down the sides again if needed. The batter should look well blended. Divide the batter between the prepared pans, smoothing it out with the rubber spatula. Place pans in the oven side by side.

BAKE the cakes until they are golden brown and spring back when lightly pressed with your finger, 27 to 29 minutes. Remove the pans from the oven and place them on wire racks to cool for 10 minutes. Run a dinner knife around the edge of each layer and invert each onto a rack, then invert them again onto another rack so that the cakes are right side up. Allow them to cool completely, 30 minutes more.

MEANWHILE, prepare the Quick Caramel Frosting.

PLACE one cake layer, right side up, on a serving platter. Spread the top with the warm frosting. Place the second layer, right side up, on top of the first layer and frost the top and sides of the cake with clean, smooth strokes. Work quickly, as the frosting will set. (If the frosting gets too hard to work with, place the pan back over low heat for 1 minute, stirring constantly, to soften it up.) Once the frosting has set, slice and serve.

NOTE: Store this cake, covered in plastic wrap or aluminum foil, at room temperature for up to 1 week. Or freeze, wrapped in foil, for up to 6 months; thaw the cake overnight on the counter before serving.

Quick Caramel Frosting

MAKES: 3 cups
PREPARATION TIME: 10 minutes

8 tablespoons (1 stick) butter
½ cup packed light brown sugar
½ cup packed dark brown sugar
¼ cup milk
2 cups confectioners' sugar, sifted
1 teaspoon pure vanilla extract

PLACE the butter and brown sugars in a medium-size heavy saucepan over medium heat. Stir and cook until the mixture comes to a boil, about 2 minutes. Add the milk, stir, and bring the mixture back to a boil, then remove the pan from the heat. Add the confectioners' sugar and

(continued on page 96)

Spice Cake Roulade

Let the glaze set for a few minutes before slicing.

NOTE: Store this cake under a glass cake dome or covered in plastic wrap at room temperature for up to 1 week. Or freeze it, wrapped in aluminum foil, for up to 6 months; thaw the cake overnight on the counter before serving.

Spice Cake Roulades

SERVES: 16
PREPARATION TIME: 35 minutes
BAKING TIME: 13 minutes
CHILL TIME: at least 30 minutes

1 package (8 ounces) cream cheese, at room temperature
1 cup confectioners' sugar, sifted
½ teaspoon vanilla extract
1 container (8 ounces) frozen whipped topping, thawed
½ cup chopped pecans or almonds, toasted
Vegetable oil cooking spray, for greasing the pans
Additional confectioners' sugar, for dusting
4 large eggs
½ cup water
1 package (18.25 ounces) plain spice cake mix
1 cup grated carrot (about 2 medium)
2 tablespoons confectioners' sugar, for garnish

FOR the filling, place the cream cheese, 1 cup confectioners' sugar, and vanilla in a large mixing bowl. Blend with an electric mixer on low speed until the ingredients are incorporated, 45 seconds. Stop the machine and add the thawed whipped topping. Beat on low until the filling is well combined and fluffy, 1 minute more. Fold in the pecans or almonds until they are well distributed. Cover the bowl with plastic wrap and set aside while preparing the cake.

PLACE a rack in the center of the oven and preheat the oven to 350°F. Lightly coat the bottom of two 15- by 10-inch jelly-roll pans with vegetable oil cooking spray and line with enough waxed paper to cover the bottoms and still have a couple of inches lapping over at

vanilla. Beat with a wooden spoon until the frosting is smooth.

USE immediately to frost the cake or the frosting will harden. If it does harden while you are frosting the cake, simply place the pan back over low heat and stir until the frosting softens up.

Fresh Orange Cake

SERVES: 16
PREPARATION TIME: 15 minutes
BAKING TIME: 45 to 47 minutes

Vegetable oil cooking spray, for misting the pan
Flour, for dusting the pan
1 package (18.25 ounces) yellow cake mix with pudding
1 cup fresh orange juice (from about 5 medium-size oranges) or from the carton
½ cup vegetable oil, such as canola, corn, safflower, soybean, or sunflower
¼ cup granulated sugar
1 teaspoon pure vanilla extract
4 large eggs
1 cup confectioners' sugar, sifted
3 tablespoons fresh orange juice (from about 1 medium-size orange)
1 teaspoon grated fresh orange zest (from about 1 medium-size orange)

PLACE a rack in the center of the oven and preheat the oven to 350°F. Lightly mist a 12-cup Bundt pan with vegetable oil cooking spray, then dust with flour. Shake out the excess flour. Set the pan aside.

PLACE the cake mix, orange juice, oil, granulated sugar, vanilla, and eggs in a large mixing bowl. Blend with an electric mixer on low speed for 1 minute. Stop the machine and scrape down the sides of the bowl with a rubber spatula. Increase the mixer speed to medium and beat for 2 minutes more, scraping down the sides again if needed. The batter should look thick and well blended. Pour the batter into the prepared pan and place it in the oven.

BAKE the cake until it is golden brown and just starts to pull away from the sides of the pan, 45 to 47 minutes. Remove the pan from the oven and place it on a wire rack to cool for 20 minutes. Run a long, sharp knife around the edge of the cake and invert it onto a rack to cool completely, 30 minutes more.

MEANWHILE, prepare the glaze. Combine the confectioners' sugar, fresh orange juice, and orange zest in a small bowl and stir with a wooden spoon until smooth.

PLACE the cake on a serving platter and pour the glaze over the top, letting it drizzle down the sides and into the center.

each end. Lightly mist the waxed paper with cooking spray, but do not spray the sides of the pan. Set the pans aside. Dust 2 clean kitchen towels with additional confectioners' sugar.

PLACE the eggs in a large mixing bowl. Beat with an electric mixer on medium-high speed for 5 minutes. Add water, beating at low speed until blended. Gradually add the cake mix, beating at low speed until moistened. Stop the machine and scrape down the sides of the bowl with a rubber spatula. Increase the mixer speed to medium-high and beat 2 minutes more. Fold in the grated carrots. Pour the batter evenly into the prepared pans, smoothing it out with the rubber spatula. Place the pans in the oven.

BAKE the cake until it springs back when lightly pressed with your finger and a toothpick inserted in the center comes out clean, 13 minutes. (If you don't have a double oven, set one pan aside.) Remove the pans from the oven and immediately invert each pan onto a prepared towel and carefully peel off the used waxed paper that clings to the bottom of the cake. While the cakes are still hot, use the towel to help carefully roll each cake into a jelly roll, or roulade. Begin with the short side next to you and roll away from you. Place the roulades, seam side down, wrapped in the kitchen towels, on cooling racks to cool for 30 minutes.

WHEN the cakes are cool, you are ready to assemble the roulades. Carefully unroll each cake, one at a time, just enough so that you can spread the inside surface generously with half the filling. Gently roll each cake back into its roulade shape, carefully pulling the kitchen towel out from under it. Place each roulade, seam side down, on a serving platter. Cover each with plastic wrap, and place the platter in the refrigerator to chill, at least 30 minutes.

BEFORE SERVING, sift 2 tablespoons confectioners' sugar over the top of the roulades. Slice into serving pieces.

NOTE: Store the roulades, covered in waxed paper, in the refrigerator for up to 4 days.

The Best Pound Cake

SERVES: 12
PREPARATION TIME: 15 minutes
BAKING TIME: 60 to 65 minutes
RESTING TIME: 40 minutes

Solid vegetable shortening, for greasing the pan
1 cup all-purpose flour, plus more for dusting the pan
8 tablespoons (1 stick) butter, at room temperature
½ cup vegetable oil
1 cup sugar
5 large eggs
1 package (18.25 ounces) plain yellow cake mix
1 container (8 ounces) sour cream, at room temperature
1 cup evaporated milk
1 tablespoon pure vanilla extract

PLACE a rack in the center of the oven and preheat the oven to 350°F.

LIGHTLY grease a 10-inch tube pan with vegetable shortening, then dust it with flour. Shake out the excess flour. Set the tube pan aside.

PLACE the butter and oil in a large mixing bowl and beat with an electric mixer on medium-low speed until creamy, 1 minute. Add the sugar and beat until creamy, 1 to 2 minutes longer. Add the eggs, 1 at a time, beating each until the yolks of the eggs have just been incorporated. Stop the machine and scrape down the sides of the bowl with a rubber spatula. Add the cake mix, the 1 cup of flour, the sour cream, evaporated milk, and vanilla. Increase the mixer speed to medium and beat until the batter is thick and well blended, 1½ to 2 minutes longer, scraping down the side of the bowl again if needed. Pour the batter into the prepared tube pan, smoothing it out with a rubber spatula.

BAKE the cake until it is golden brown and springs back when lightly pressed with a finger, 60 to 65 minutes. Remove the tube pan from the oven and place it on a wire rack to cool for 20 minutes. Run a dinner knife around the edge of the cake, shake it gently to loosen it, and invert it onto a rack; then invert it again onto another rack so that the

Q&A for the Cake Mix Doctor

Q What happens if I pick the wrong pan size?

A If the pan is too big, the cake will take less time to bake and may shrink back while baking. If the pan is too small, the cake will take more time to bake and may rise over the sides of the pan.

Q Are you always supposed to grease a pan before baking a cake?

A Not always. Roulades and angel food cakes call for ungreased sides so the batter can reach up and cling to the side of the pan and not slide back down.

Q What are the holes and tunnels in my baked cake?

A They are round- or sausage-shaped air bubbles trapped in the cake batter. To get rid of them, either sharply tap the filled cake pan several times on the kitchen counter before you place it in the oven or run a knife through the batter in zigzag motions to pop the bubbles. You can avoid tunneling by not overbeating the cake-mix batter or not beating it at too high a mixer speed.

Q How can I cut neat slices from a frosted cake?

A Moisten the knife blade completely with hot water before each cut, then dry it well. Once you've made a cut, wipe the knife clean with a paper towel and remoisten in hot water. Repeat the process to cut each slice.

cake is right side up. Allow the cake to cool completely, 20 minutes longer.

NOTE: Store this cake, loosely covered with plastic wrap or in a cake saver, at room temperature for up to 1 week. Or freeze it, wrapped in aluminum foil, for up to 6 months; thaw overnight in the refrigerator before serving.

Pies and Pastries in the Nick of Time

You'll be slicing up perfect pies and pastries in no time with these easy recipes.

Cream Cheese Brownie Pie

SERVES: 8
PREPARATION TIME: 15 minutes
BAKING TIME: 40 to 45 minutes
ASSEMBLY TIME: 2 minutes

1 store-bought refrigerated 9-inch pie
   crust
1 package (8 ounces) cream cheese,
   at room temperature
3 tablespoons sugar
1 teaspoon pure vanilla extract
3 large eggs
1 package (15.1 ounces) hot fudge
   swirl deluxe brownie mix
¼ cup vegetable oil
2 tablespoons water
½ cup chopped pecans

PLACE a rack in the center of the oven and preheat the oven to 350°F. Place the pie crust in a 9-inch pie pan. Flute the edges as desired.
PLACE the cream cheese, sugar, vanilla, and 1 egg in a medium-size mixing bowl. Blend with an electric mixer on low speed until smooth, 1 minute. Set the bowl aside.
SET aside the hot fudge packet from the brownie mix (you'll use it for the topping). Place the brownie mix, oil, 1 tablespoon of the water, and the remaining 2 eggs in a large mixing bowl. Beat with a wooden spoon until just incorporated and smooth, about 50 strokes. Spread ½ cup of the brownie mixture in the bottom of the crust. Spoon teaspoonfuls of the cream cheese

mixture over this and spread it over the brownie layer with a rubber spatula. Top with the remaining brownie mixture, spreading it evenly to smooth the top. Sprinkle the pecans on top of the pie. Place the pan in the oven.
BAKE the pie until the crust is deep golden brown, the center has puffed up, and the nuts have toasted, 40 to 45 minutes. Remove the pan from the oven and place it on a wire rack to cool.
BEFORE serving, squirt the reserved hot fudge sauce from the packet into a small glass bowl. Place in the microwave oven on high power to warm, 30 seconds. Stir in the remaining 1 tablespoon water. Serve the pie warm or place in the refrigerator, uncovered, until chilled, 3 hours. Slice the pie and drizzle the fudge sauce over each slice.

NOTE: Store this pie, covered in aluminum foil, in the refrigerator for up to 1 week. Or freeze it, wrapped in foil, for up to 2 months; thaw the pie overnight in the refrigerator before serving.

Kentucky Bourbon-Pecan Fudge Pie

SERVES: 8
PREPARATION TIME: 10 minutes
BAKING TIME: 42 to 47 minutes

1 store-bought refrigerated 9-inch pie
   crust
1 package (19.8 ounces) brownie mix
8 tablespoons (1 stick) unsalted
   butter, melted
¼ cup bourbon, buttermilk, or water
2 large eggs
½ cup semisweet chocolate chips
¼ cup finely chopped pecans

PLACE a rack in the center of the oven and preheat the oven to 350°F. Place the pie crust in a 9-inch pie pan. Flute the edges as desired.

Cream Cheese Brownie Pie

PLACE the brownie mix, melted butter, bourbon, and eggs in a large mixing bowl. Beat with a wooden spoon until just incorporated and smooth, about 50 strokes. Pour the batter onto the prepared crust, smoothing the top with a rubber spatula. Sprinkle the chocolate chips and pecans on top of the pie. Place the pie in the oven.

BAKE the pie until the crust is deep golden brown, the center has puffed up, and the nuts have toasted, 42 to 47 minutes. Remove the pan from the oven and place it on a wire rack to cool for 30 minutes. Slice and serve.

NOTE: Store this pie, covered in aluminum foil, at room temperature for up to 3 days or in the refrigerator for up to 1 week. Or freeze it, wrapped in foil, for up to 2 months; thaw the pie overnight in the refrigerator before serving.

Apple Walnut Crisp

SERVES: 18 to 20
PREPARATION TIME: 12 minutes
BAKING TIME: 55 to 60 minutes

2 cans (21 ounces each) apple pie filling
1 lemon
1 teaspoon ground cinnamon
1 package (18.25 ounces) plain yellow cake mix
1 cup chopped walnuts
1 cup (2 sticks) butter, melted
Vanilla ice cream, for serving

PLACE a rack in the center of the oven and preheat the oven to 350°F.

SPOON the apple pie filling evenly onto the bottom of an ungreased 13- by 9-inch baking pan. Grate the zest from the lemon and sprinkle it over the apples. Cut the lemon in half and squeeze the juice over the apples. Sprinkle the apples with ½ teaspoon of the cinnamon. Pour the dry cake mix evenly over the apples so that it reaches all the sides of the pan. Sprinkle the cake mix with the remaining ½ teaspoon cinnamon. Sprinkle the walnuts on top and drizzle the melted butter over the entire pan. Place the pan in the oven.

BAKE the crisp until it is golden brown and bubbly and the walnuts have

browned, 55 to 60 minutes. Remove the pan from the oven and place it on a wire rack to cool for 10 minutes.

SPOON the crisp into bowls, top with a scoop of vanilla ice cream, and serve.

NOTE: Store this crisp, covered in plastic wrap, for up to 1 day in the refrigerator if using a metal pan, or for up to 1 week if using a glass pan. If using a metal pan, let the crisp cool, then transfer it to a glass or plastic container; it will keep, covered, for up to 1 week in the refrigerator.

Sour Cream-Pear Buckle

SERVES: 18 to 20
PREPARATION TIME: 15 minutes
BAKING TIME: 45 to 50 minutes

Solid vegetable shortening, for greasing the pan
Flour, for dusting the pan
1 package (18.25 ounces) plain yellow cake mix
4 tablespoons (½ stick) butter, melted
2 large eggs
½ teaspoon ground cinnamon
5 medium-size pears, peeled, cored, and sliced ¼ inch thick (5 cups sliced)
½ cup packed light brown sugar
½ cup chopped pecans or raisins
½ teaspoon ground cinnamon
1 cup sour cream
1 large egg
1 teaspoon pure vanilla extract

PLACE a rack in the center of the oven and preheat the oven to 350°F. Lightly grease a 13- by 9-inch baking pan with solid vegetable shortening, then dust with flour. Shake out excess flour. Set the pan aside.

PLACE the cake mix, melted butter, eggs, and cinnamon in a large mixing bowl. Blend with an electric mixer on low speed until the mixture just comes together into a stiff dough, 1 minute. Using wet fingertips, press the dough evenly over the bottom of the prepared pan so that it reaches the sides of the pan. Set the pan aside.

PLACE the pear slices in a medium-size

(continued on page 100)

glass mixing bowl and place in the microwave oven. Cook, uncovered, on high power for 2 minutes. Remove the bowl and stir the pear slices. Return the bowl to the microwave and cook on high power for 2 minutes more. Remove the bowl and pour the pears over the crust, spreading them evenly with a spoon. Sprinkle the brown sugar over the pears. Sprinkle the nuts and cinnamon over the brown sugar.

FOR the topping, place the sour cream, egg, and vanilla in a small mixing bowl. Whisk to combine, then pour the mixture over the top of the cake so that it has a drizzled effect and isn't spread neatly from edge to edge. Place the pan in the oven.

BAKE the cake until the sour cream topping firms up and the cake springs back when lightly pressed with your finger, 45 to 50 minutes. Remove the pan from the oven and place it on a wire rack to cool for 20 minutes.

SLICE the warm buckle into pieces and, using a metal spatula, remove them from the pan to a serving platter. Serve warm.

NOTE: Store this cake, covered in plastic wrap, in the refrigerator up to 1 week. Or freeze it, wrapped in aluminum foil, for up to 6 months. Before serving, open the foil and reheat the cake in a preheated 300°F oven until warmed through.

15 ways to doctor frozen pies

REAL WHIPPED CREAM MAKES ANY PIE TASTE HOMEMADE. Flavor whipped cream with powdered sugar and vanilla. Try a pinch of cinnamon or cocoa powder if you're feeling adventurous.

APPLE PIE

1 Brush the top crust with a beaten egg and cinnamon sugar before baking.

2 Top with shredded Cheddar cheese and toasted pecans after baking.

3 After baking, glaze the pie with melted apple jelly for that French bakery look. Sprinkle with sliced toasted almonds.

4 Drizzle the top with butterscotch sauce after baking.

5 After baking, drizzle with a glaze made of confectioners' sugar and a little milk. Add vanilla and maybe cinnamon to taste.

PUMPKIN OR SWEET POTATO PIE

6 Dollop with marshmallow creme or use miniature marshmallows, and run the pie under the broiler until bubbly and golden brown.

7 Sprinkle the top with freshly grated nutmeg before baking.

8 After baking, glaze with melted orange marmalade.

9 Before baking, ring the pie crust with pecan halves.

10 Sprinkle with a crumb mixture of brown sugar, butter, and chopped pecans during the last 15 minutes of baking.

11 Before baking, sprinkle with chopped pecan pralines.

PECAN PIE

12 Dress it up with a layer of chocolate chips. Toss them on during the last 15 minutes of baking.

13 Brush with bourbon after baking or serve with a bourbon-scented whipped cream.

14 Serve slices over pools of custard sauce made by melting a good quality vanilla bean ice cream.

15 Shave white and dark chocolate curls by running a potato peeler over a bar of chocolate. Sprinkle over the pie before serving.

Fresh Lime Cheesecake

SERVES: 20
PREPARATION TIME: 15 minutes
BAKING TIME: 45 to 50 minutes
CHILL TIME: at least 1 hour

Softened butter or solid vegetable shortening, for greasing the pan
1 package (18.25 ounces) plain yellow cake mix
4 tablespoons (½ stick) butter, melted
4 large eggs
2 packages (8 ounces each) cream cheese, at room temperature
1 can (14 ounces) sweetened condensed milk
1 tablespoon grated fresh lime zest
½ cup fresh lime juice (from 3 to 5 regular limes or 6 to 10 Key limes)
1 cup Sweetened Cream or frozen whipped topping, thawed, for serving

PLACE a rack in the center of the oven and preheat the oven to 325°F. Lightly grease a 13- by 9-inch baking pan with the softened butter or vegetable shortening. Set the pan aside.

MEASURE out ½ cup of the cake mix and set aside for the filling.

PLACE the remaining cake mix, the melted butter, and 1 egg in a large mixing bowl. Blend with an electric mixer on low speed for 2 minutes. Stop the machine, and scrape down the sides of the bowl with a rubber spatula. The batter should come together in a ball. With your fingertips, pat the batter evenly over the bottom and 1 inch up the sides of the prepared pan, smoothing it out with your fingers until the top is smooth. Set the pan aside.

FOR the filling, place the cream cheese and the sweetened condensed milk in the same mixing bowl that was used to make the crust and with the same beaters blend with an electric mixer on low speed until just combined, 30 seconds. Stop the machine; add the reserved ½ cup cake mix, the remaining 3 eggs, the lime zest, and lime juice and beat on medium speed for 1 minute. Stop the machine; scrape down the sides of the bowl with a rubber spatula. Pour the filling onto the crust; spread with the rubber spatula so that the filling covers the entire surface and reaches the sides of the pan. Place the pan in the oven.

BAKE the cheesecake until it looks shiny and the center no longer jiggles when you shake the pan, 45 to 50 minutes. Remove the pan from the oven and place it on a wire rack to cool, 30 minutes. Lightly cover the pan with plastic wrap and place the pan in the refrigerator to chill for at least 1 hour, but preferably 24 hours for the flavors to meld. Cut into squares and serve with a dollop of Sweetened Cream.

NOTE: Store this cake, covered in plastic wrap or aluminum foil, in the refrigerator for up to 1 week. Or freeze it, wrapped in foil, for up to 2 months; thaw the cake overnight in the refrigerator before serving.

Sweetened Cream

MAKES: 2 cups
PREPARATION TIME: 4 minutes

1 cup heavy (whipping) cream
¼ cup confectioners' sugar, sifted,
    or to taste
½ teaspoon pure vanilla extract or
    pure almond extract

CHILL a large, clean mixing bowl and electric mixer beaters in the freezer for a few minutes while you assemble the ingredients.

POUR the cream into the chilled bowl and beat with the electric mixer on high speed until it thickens, 1½ minutes. Stop the machine and add the confectioners' sugar and the vanilla extract. Beat the cream on high speed until stiff peaks form, 1 to 2 minutes more. Chill until ready to serve.

Pumpkin Spice Cheesecake

SERVES: 20
PREPARATION TIME: 15 minutes
BAKING TIME: 47 to 55 minutes
CHILL TIME: at least 1 hour

Softened butter or solid vegetable
    shortening, for greasing the pan
1 package (18.25 ounces) plain spice
    cake mix
4 tablespoons (½ stick) butter, melted
4 large eggs

2 packages (8 ounces each) cream
    cheese, at room temperature
1 can (14 ounces) sweetened
    condensed milk
1 cup canned pumpkin
½ cup packed light brown sugar
½ teaspoon ground cinnamon
¼ teaspoon ground nutmeg
¼ teaspoon ground ginger
1 cup sour cream
¼ cup packed light brown sugar

PLACE a rack in the center of the oven and preheat the oven to 325°F. Lightly grease a 13- by 9-inch baking pan with the softened butter or vegetable shortening. Set the pan aside.

MEASURE out ½ cup of the cake mix and set aside for the filling.

PLACE the remaining cake mix, melted butter, and 1 egg in a large mixing bowl. Blend with an electric mixer on low speed for 2 minutes. Stop the machine and scrape down the sides of the bowl with a rubber spatula. The batter should come together in a ball. With your fingertips, pat the batter evenly over the bottom of the prepared pan, smoothing it out with your fingers until the top is smooth. Set the pan aside.

FOR the filling, place the cream cheese and the sweetened condensed milk in the same mixing bowl that was used to make the crust and with the same beaters (no need to clean either) blend with an electric mixer on low speed until just combined, 30 seconds. Stop the

machine and add the reserved cake mix, the remaining 3 eggs, the pumpkin, brown sugar, cinnamon, nutmeg, and ginger and beat on medium speed for 1 minute. Stop the machine and scrape down the sides of the bowl with the rubber spatula. Pour the filling onto the crust and spread with the rubber spatula so that the filling covers the entire surface and reaches the sides of the pan. Place the pan in the oven.

BAKE the cheesecake until it looks shiny and the center no longer jiggles when you shake the pan, 40 to 45 minutes. Remove the pan from the oven while you prepare the topping. Leave the oven on.

FOR the topping, place the sour cream and brown sugar in a small mixing bowl and stir with a spoon until well combined. Pour the topping over the cheesecake and return the pan to the oven.

BAKE until the topping sets, 7 to 10 minutes. Remove the pan from the oven and place it on a wire rack to cool, 30 minutes. Lightly cover the pan with plastic wrap and place the pan in the refrigerator to chill for at least 1 hour, but preferably 24 hours for the flavors to meld. Cut into bars and serve.

NOTE: Store cake, covered in plastic wrap or aluminum foil, in the refrigerator for up to 1 week. Or freeze it, wrapped in foil, for up to 2 months; thaw overnight in the refrigerator before serving.

Pumpkin Spice Cheesecake

Double Chocolate
Chewies

Visions of Sugarplums

You don't have to merely dream of these cookies and candies.
They're easy to make and even sweeter to eat.

Double Chocolate Chewies

MAKES: 42 cookies
PREPARATION TIME: 5 minutes
BAKING TIME: 10 to 12 minutes per batch

... food cake mix
⅓ cup water
4 tablespoons (½ stick) butter, melted
1 large egg
1 bag (6 ounces; 1 cup) semisweet chocolate chips
½ cup chopped walnuts, pecans, or hazelnuts

PLACE a rack in the center of the oven and preheat the oven to 350°F. Lightly grease two cookie sheets with solid vegetable shortening. Set the pans aside.

PLACE the cake mix, water, melted butter, and egg in a large mixing bowl. Blend with an electric mixer on low speed for 1 minute. Stop the machine and scrape down the sides of the bowl with a rubber spatula. Increase the speed to medium and beat for 1 minute more. The cookie dough will be thick. Fold in the chips and nuts until well distributed.

DROP heaping teaspoonfuls of the dough 2 inches apart on the prepared cookie sheets. Place the pans in the oven. (If your oven cannot accommodate both pans on the center rack, place one sheet on the top rack and one on the center rack and rotate them halfway through the baking time.)

BAKE the cookies until they have set but are still a little soft in the center, 10 to 12 minutes. Remove the pans from the oven. Let the cookies rest on the cookie sheets for 1 minute. Remove the cookies with a metal spatula to wire racks to cool completely, 20 minutes. Repeat the baking process with the remaining cookie dough.

NOTE: Store the cookies, wrapped in aluminum foil or in an airtight container, at room temperature for up to 1 week. Or freeze them, wrapped in foil and placed in a plastic freezer bag, for up to 2 months.

MAKES: 2 dozen
PREPARATION TIME: 15 minutes
BAKING TIME: 28 to 30 minutes

Vegetable oil cooking spray, for misting the pan
1 package (18.25 ounces) plain German chocolate cake mix
12 tablespoons (1½ sticks) butter, at room temperature
1 can (5 ounces) evaporated milk
1 bag (14 ounces) caramels (45 small caramels), unwrapped
1 to 2 cups semisweet chocolate chips
1 cup chopped walnuts or pecans (optional)

PLACE a rack in the center of the oven and preheat the oven to 350°F. Lightly mist the bottom of a 13- by 9-inch pan with vegetable oil cooking spray. Set the pan aside.

PLACE the cake mix, butter, and ⅓ cup of the evaporated milk in a large mixing bowl. Blend with an electric mixer on low speed for 1 minute. The batter will be thick and well combined. Turn half of the batter into the prepared pan, smoothing it out with a rubber spatula. Place the pan in the oven.

BAKE the cake layer until it puffs up but is still soft, 6 minutes. Remove the pan from the oven. Leave the oven on.

PLACE the caramels in a medium-size saucepan with the remaining ⅓ cup evaporated milk. Stir and cook over medium-low heat until the caramels melt and the mixture is smooth and

(continued on page 104)

---

top 10 cookie secrets

... make good substitutes.

2 **Keep the mixing of the dough to a minimum.** Stir just until the flour disappears; overmixing toughens the dough.

3 **Lightly grease the cookie sheets only if the recipe specifies,** then use only vegetable oil cooking spray or solid shortening. Butter encourages burning.

4 **Use shiny, heavy aluminum cookie sheets for baking.** Dark sheets may cause the cookies to brown too much on the bottom, and insulated sheets require slightly longer baking. Nonstick sheets work well if they're not too dark.

5 **Use a teaspoon** (not a measuring spoon) to pick up drop cookie dough and another teaspoon to push the dough onto the cookie sheet.

6 **When baking brownies,** line a lightly greased pan with aluminum foil before spreading the batter in the pan. When done, simply lift the foil along with the uncut brownies out of the pan, remove foil, and easily cut the brownies.

7 **Check for doneness** at the minimum baking time to promote even browning.

8 **Transfer baked cookies to a wire rack immediately** unless recipe directs otherwise.

9 **Allow the cookie sheets to cool** before reusing.

10 **If you're short on wire racks,** place a sheet of waxed paper on the counter and sprinkle with sugar. Then transfer the cookies from the cookie sheet to the sugared paper. The cookies will cool without getting soggy.

I can't recall a Christmas when there weren't Rum Balls nudging the sugar cookies for space on the cookie platter.

thick, 4 to 5 minutes. Remove the pan from the heat and pour the hot caramel mixture over the cake layer. Scatter the chocolate chips evenly on top. Dollop teaspoonfuls of the remaining cake batter at random over the chocolate chips. Scatter the nuts on top of the batter if desired. Place the pan in the oven. **BAKE** until the batter on top lightly browns and a crust forms around the edges of the pan, 22 to 24 minutes. The brownies should still be a little soft in the center. Remove the pan from the oven and place it on a wire rack to cool completely, 30 minutes.

SLICE and serve the brownies. To make slicing easier, chill the brownies 1 hour.

NOTE: Store these brownies, covered with plastic wrap or aluminum foil, at room temperature for up to 3 days or in the refrigerator for up to 1 week. Or freeze them, wrapped in foil, for up to 6 months; thaw the brownies overnight on the counter before serving.

Rum Balls

MAKES: 3 dozen
PREPARATION TIME: 10 minutes
BAKING TIME: 30 minutes

One half of an angel food cake, baked
    in a 10-inch round tube pan
1 cup (2 sticks) butter, at room
    temperature
6 cups confectioners' sugar, sifted
½ cup light rum
1 pound pecans, finely ground

CUT the cooled angel food cake into 6 slices, then cut each slice into 6 squares, 1½ inches each. Discard any scraps. Set aside.

PLACE the butter in a large mixing bowl. Blend with an electric mixer on low speed until creamy, 1 minute. Gradually add the confectioners' sugar, blending on low speed for 1 minute. Stop the machine and scrape down the sides of the bowl with a rubber spatula. Add

half the rum, then blend again on low speed for 1 minute, adding more of the remaining rum until you get the right spreading consistency, soft like frosting but not runny. Set aside.

SPREAD out the ground pecans in a shallow pie pan or wide glass dish.

SPREAD rum frosting generously on all sides of the cake squares, then lightly dredge the squares in the ground pecans. Transfer the rum balls in one layer to waxed paper-lined cookie tins or plastic storage containers to chill before serving.

NOTE: Store the rum balls, wrapped in waxed paper in a tin or plastic airtight storage container, in the refrigerator for up to 2 weeks.

Chunky Chocolate-Peanut Bars

MAKES: 4 dozen
PREPARATION TIME: 20 minutes
BAKING TIME: 25 to 30 minutes

1 package (18.25 ounces) plain yellow
    cake mix
1 cup chunky peanut butter
8 tablespoons (1 stick) butter, melted
2 large eggs
2 cups semisweet chocolate chips
1 can (14 ounces) sweetened
    condensed milk
2 tablespoons (¼ stick) butter
1 cup frozen unsweetened grated
    coconut, thawed, or sweetened
    flaked coconut
2 teaspoons pure vanilla extract

PLACE a rack in the center of the oven and preheat the oven to 325°F. Set aside an ungreased 13- by 9-inch baking pan.

PLACE the cake mix, peanut butter, melted butter, and eggs in a large mixing bowl. Blend with an electric mixer on low speed for 1 minute. Stop the machine and scrape down the sides of the bowl with a rubber spatula. The mixture will be satiny and thick.

Rum Balls

Chunky Chocolate-Peanut Bars

Reserve 1½ cups of the mixture for the topping. Transfer the remaining mixture to the pan. Using your fingertips, press the mixture evenly over the bottom of the pan so that it reaches the sides. Set aside.

FOR the filling, place the chocolate chips, condensed milk, and 2 tablespoons butter in a medium-size heavy saucepan over low heat. Stir and cook until the chocolate is melted and the mixture is well combined, 3 to 4 minutes. Remove the pan from the heat and stir in the coconut and vanilla until well distributed. Pour the chocolate mixture over the crust and spread it evenly with the rubber spatula so that it reaches the sides of the pan. Using your fingertips, crumble the reserved crust mixture and scatter it evenly over the chocolate. Place the pan in the oven.

BAKE the cake until it is light brown, 25 to 30 minutes. Remove the pan from the oven and place it on a wire rack to cool completely.

CUT into 48 bars. Remove the bars from the pan with a metal spatula and serve.

NOTE: Store these bars, covered in plastic wrap or aluminum foil, at room temperature for up to 3 days or in the refrigerator for up to 1 week. Or freeze them, wrapped in foil, for up to 6 months; thaw the bars overnight on the counter before serving.

Cake Mix Oatmeal Cookies

MAKES: 5 dozen
PREPARATION TIME: 15 minutes
BAKING TIME: 12 minutes per batch

1 package (18.25 ounce) plain yellow
    cake mix
2 cups quick-cooking oats, uncooked
1 cup sugar
1 cup vegetable oil
2 large eggs
1 cup chopped pecans
1½ teaspoons vanilla extract

PLACE a rack in the center of the oven and preheat the oven to 350°F. Set aside two ungreased cookie sheets.

PLACE the cake mix, oats, and sugar in a large bowl. Combine the oil and the eggs and add to the dry ingredients, stirring well. Stir in the pecans and vanilla extract.

DROP rounded teaspoonfuls of the dough 2 inches apart on the cookie sheets. Place the pans in the oven. (If your oven cannot accommodate both pans on the center rack, place one sheet on the top rack and one on the center rack and rotate them halfway through the baking time.)

BAKE the cookies for 12 minutes or until lightly browned. Remove the pans from the oven, then remove the cookies with a metal spatula to wire racks to cool completely. Repeat the baking process with the remaining cookie dough.

Holiday Planning Guide

Breeze through the holidays with these expert decorating, cooking, and party tips from the Cake Mix Doctor.

Fast & Festive Decorating

• **SHOWCASE ORNAMENTS** in a glass bowl for an easy, no-maintenance centerpiece.

• **GATHER MISCELLANEOUS DISHES** from around your house, fill them with jelly beans or chocolate candies, and tuck a handwritten note in each dish with a word of holiday cheer (such as "Rejoice!").

• **PLACE SEVERAL CLOVE-SPIKED ORANGES** in a bright bowl in your kitchen to create a refreshing holiday scent.

• **GATHER BACKYARD EVERGREEN CUTTINGS** to use anywhere holiday spirit is needed. Allow cut stems to soak in water overnight before arranging. Display in vases and accent with pinecones, berries, and fresh fruit.

holiday touches for the table

• **Write guests' names and the date on plain ornaments using a paint pen.** Use the personalized ornaments as place cards and party favors.

• **Stack small, wrapped packages containing party favors on a cake stand or scatter them across the tabletop.** After the meal, each guest can choose a gift from the assortment for a take-home treasure.

• **Tuck napkins and flatware into colorful mittens.** The pairs of mittens double as place favors.

Silver Shortcuts

• **WHEN SERVING FOOD IN SILVER PIECES,** use a glass bowl or liner to prevent acidic foods (such as tomatoes, citrus fruit, and mayonnaise) from coming in contact with silver. Also, remember that salt pits silver.

• **DO NOT SCRAPE WAX OFF A SILVER CANDLESTICK WITH A SHARP OBJECT**—you may damage the finish. Instead, place the candlestick in the freezer to harden wax and then gently chip it off with your fingernail.

• **POLISHING MITTS AND CLOTHS** designed specifically for silver care are convenient for removing light tarnish. Polishing mitts, cloths, and tarnish strips usually can be found where silver polish is sold and at large housewares stores.

• **OLD TOOTHBRUSHES AND PAPER TOWELS** are not good substitutes for polishing cloths because they might mar the finish.

• **STORE SILVER WITH TARNISH-PREVENTIVE SILVER STRIPS.** Placing silver in a sealed zipper-lock plastic bag should give you about six months of tarnish protection.

• **WHEN SILVER IS DEEPLY TARNISHED, RESIST THE URGE TO TRY A "MIRACLE DIP."** Silver dips remove the tarnish, but they often take off the finish and give the piece a greenish yellow appearance. Take heavily tarnished pieces to a reputable jewelry or silver shop for a professional cleaning. Remember, a deep tarnish in crevices on ornate silver actually adds character!

• **USE YOUR SILVER!** The pieces only get better with use.

Party Essentials

• **ORGANIZE A PARTY CLOSET** filled with all the items you'll need for holiday activities. With a well-stocked closet, you'll be set for a season of easy entertaining.

• **CENTERPIECES.** Have at least one pretty container, such as a tureen or trifle dish, for the base of a centerpiece. In a pinch, a glass trifle dish filled with fruit makes an easy, last-minute centerpiece.

• **FABRIC AND RIBBONS.** Purchase a few yards of fabrics in holiday hues to swirl loosely down the center of the table. There's no need to hem the edges; just iron them under. Use coordinating ribbons to tie up napkins and flatware for easy handling.

• **VOTIVE CANDLEHOLDERS.** Collect these by the dozen, and you'll have enough to spread a Christmassy glow all through the house—on the dining table, along the mantel, and in the guest bath.

• **SERVING PIECES.** For casual entertaining, use baskets for easy cleanup. Select colorful holiday napkins or tea towels to use as basket liners. Large bowls make entertaining easy because you don't have to refill them very often. White serving pieces are good choices—they complement various food items and coordinate well with predominantly white dinner plates.

• **FOR BEVERAGES.** You'll need an ice bucket and tongs. Wine carafes make attractive serving pitchers. A large coffeepot makes it easy to accommodate serving a group. Consider purchasing a pot jointly with a neighbor—then you can take turns using it.

Christmas Dinner Stress-Savers

• **THIS TIME OF YEAR, REFRIGERATOR STORAGE SPACE IS AT A PREMIUM, SO START A NEW HOLIDAY RITUAL**—a weekly refrigerator cleaning. Designate a day (the day before trash pickup is a good choice) to reclaim refrigerator space from old leftovers and expired items and to make room for special seasonal dishes.

• **PLAN AHEAD.** Have the table set, flowers arranged, and anything non-food-related done the day before so you can devote your time to enjoying the food, family, and guests during the celebration.

• **DESIGNATE AN AREA FOR BEVERAGES.** This allows guests to serve themselves, creating opportunities for them to make themselves at home and freeing you to tend to other duties.

• **IDENTIFY SERVING PIECES AND UTENSILS FOR EACH DISH AHEAD OF TIME.** Place a slip of paper with the name of the recipe to be served on each piece. You'll save yourself from that last-minute rush to find your favorite serving platter.

• **PREPARE AS MANY RECIPES AHEAD OF TIME AS POSSIBLE.** Write out the baking or reheating instructions and tape them to the cover of the dish. Not only will this reduce the stress of last minute food-preparation, but also it will eliminate cookbook clutter and the mountain of pots and pans in the sink when guests arrive.

• **CLEAN UP AS YOU GO.** Start the party with an empty trash can and an empty dishwasher; wash pots and pans as you use them.

White Christmas

Group a variety of white blooming plants or cut flowers for a dramatic wintry display. Choose several shapes and sizes. There are many possibilities to choose from, such as poinsettias, paperwhites, crocus, and baby's breath. Unify the grouping by using similar containers throughout.

Kitchen Time-Cutters

• **MEASURE DRY INGREDIENTS BEFORE MOIST ONES** to minimize cleanup. Before measuring honey and other sticky ingredients, rinse the measure with hot water; then the honey will slide right out.

• **CHOP DRY INGREDIENTS, SUCH AS BREAD CRUMBS OR NUTS, IN A FOOD PROCESSOR FIRST.** Then chop or shred moist or wet foods without washing the work bowl.

• **USE A FOOD PROCESSOR TO CHOP, SLICE, OR SHRED** several ingredients consecutively or together without washing the work bowl if the ingredients will be combined later.

• **CHOP AND FREEZE ½-CUP PORTIONS** of green bell pepper, onion, and parsley in zipper-lock plastic freezer bags or purchase prepackaged frozen chopped onions and green bell peppers. When you have extra time, prepare dry bread crumbs, shredded cheese, and toasted nuts to freeze.

• **BUY INGREDIENTS IN CLOSEST-TO-USABLE FORM.** Choose such items as skinned and boned chicken breasts, peeled shrimp, and shredded cheese. Select bags of precut produce at your supermarket or purchase ready-made ingredients at the salad bar.

• **WHEN SLICING VEGETABLES** such as carrots, green onions, or celery, slice three or four pieces at a time.

• **CUT VEGETABLES INTO SMALL PIECES** or thin slices to cook faster.

• **SUBSTITUTE AN EQUAL AMOUNT** of ready-to-serve chicken broth for homemade chicken stock.

Make It . . . Quick & Easy

• **USE A PIZZA CUTTER** to cut dough or to cut day-old bread into cubes for croutons—it's faster than a knife.

• **TO MAKE CRACKER CRUMBS OR COOKIE CRUMBS** without a food processor, place crackers or cookies in a zipper-lock plastic freezer bag; roll with a rolling pin or pound with a meat mallet.

microwave shortcuts

MELTING BUTTER

Place butter in a microwave-safe glass measure; microwave at high power until melted.

1 to 2 tablespoons	**20 to 30 seconds**
¼ to ½ cup	**40 to 50 seconds**
¾ cup	**50 to 60 seconds**
1 cup	**1 to 1½ minutes**

SOFTENING BUTTER

Place butter in a microwave-safe measure or on a plate; microwave at low power (10%) until softened.

1 to 2 tablespoons	**10 to 30 seconds**
¼ to ½ cup	**30 seconds to 1 minute**
1 cup	**1 to 1½ minutes**

NOTE: Time ranges are given for 750-watt and 1,000-watt ovens, starting with cold butter.

Christmas Cleanup Tips

• **WHILE ENTERTAINING FOR THE HOLIDAYS,** keep a disaster kit handy. To deal with the inevitable spills, have paper towels, a couple of small plastic trash bags, and club soda stashed strategically. A splash of club soda followed by a quick blotting with a paper towel often prevents a small spill from becoming a major stain.

• **OPENING PRESENTS IS A JOYOUS FAMILY ACTIVITY,** but it can produce a generous pile of boxes, tissue paper, and gift wrap. To make short work of taming the mess, have a couple of large trash bags handy. Resist the temptation to burn wrapping paper in the fireplace; the colored inks can release toxic fumes when burned, and smoldering paper can blow out of the chimney, creating a fire hazard.

holiday party countdown

A GOOD PARTY PLAN MAKES EVERYTHING GO MORE SMOOTHLY ON THE BIG DAY. Our countdown helps you begin your preparations up to six weeks ahead of your event.

4 TO 6 WEEKS AHEAD

- **Set the date and time.**
- **Make your guest list.**
- **Decide what you'll serve.** Consult make-ahead recipe notes. On your calendar, write when you'll prepare or assemble each dish. Order any food you decide to have catered.
- **Select invitations** if you plan to send them for your party.

3 WEEKS AHEAD

- **Mail party invitations.** For informal events, send invitations two weeks in advance.

1 TO 2 WEEKS AHEAD

- **Check your supply of chairs, serving dishes, flatware, and glassware.**
- **Make a grocery list.** Shop for nonperishables.
- **Give some thought to your home's exterior.** Plant seasonal flowers in a planter on the front porch, hang a festive wreath, wash front-facing windows—anything to give your place a lift.

2 TO 3 DAYS AHEAD

- **Get out china, serving dishes, and utensils.** Polish silver.
- **Shop for perishables.**
- **Clean house.** If you're too busy, consider hiring a cleaning crew.
- **Make place cards.**

1 DAY AHEAD

- **Plan a centerpiece.** Buy flowers or clip greenery and berries from your backyard.
- **Prepare dishes that can be made ahead.**
- **Chill beverages. Make extra ice.**
- **Anticipate "guest geography."** Arrange furniture to maximize seating, pulling service chairs from other rooms. Place occasional or folding tables nearby.

DAY OF THE EVENT

- **Set the table.** Arrange the centerpiece.
- **Finish preparing food and arrange it on serving dishes.** For a buffet or large party, fill additional trays so that you can replenish the table by exchanging a full tray for an empty one.
- **Reserve some time for rest.** If you're refreshed and relaxed, you'll be able to enjoy your party every bit as much as your guests will.

index

Entrées

Salads

Sandwiches

Sauces and Seasonings

Soups, Chilis, Chowders, and Stews

Vegetable Sides

Top 10 Things to Remember
About the Holidays

The holidays are a joyous but often frantic time, so keep in mind my top 10 tips for the season.

10 PLAN AHEAD. Do you want to maintain Christmas traditions or add something different this year? Or maybe you want to shift the focus from shopping to the religious significance Christmas holds? We try to place church events on our calendar first and then include other activities with family and close friends.

9 MAKE LISTS. I don't know what I would do without yellow legal pads and sticky notes. And be sure to enlist help! Let others bring a dish to get-togethers or clean up afterward. You'll find enormous peace in the realization that even if you *are* organized, you don't have to do it alone.

8 DECORATE THE INSIDE OF YOUR HOME, BUT KEEP IT SIMPLE. Fresh greenery goes a long way in making the mantel, stair railings, doorways, and windows festive.

7 LIGHT THE OUTSIDE. String lights on shrubs and small trees, as well as around the top of the front door. Place a pretty green wreath with a bow on the door. Our children make luminarias by filling paper lunch sacks with sand, nestling a white votive candle in each, and then placing them along the front pathway to our door.

6 YOUR NOSE KNOWS. Simmer whole cinnamon sticks and cloves in water; or make a quick mulled cider by simmering these spices in apple cider and serve the delicious beverage in punch cups. In a pinch, buy holiday potpourri and place throughout the house.

5 CAPTURE THE MOMENTS. Take photos and shoot videos of your gatherings. We love to group our first cousins together each year for a photo, and we always snap a picture of our children on the front steps. It's fun to look back and see how we all have aged so gracefully!

4 HONOR THE PAST. Food traditions are more important than culinary trends. Make your grandmother's ambrosia. Serve family-favorite scalloped oysters. Or bake the orange layer cake you remember eating as a child.

3 BE OPEN TO CHANGE. Invite friends, neighbors, or coworkers who might not have family nearby to dine with you. We find that as extended families become more fragmented, it's more difficult for people to get together with loved ones every year.

2 THANK GOODNESS FOR SHORTCUTS. Everything doesn't have to be made from scratch. Use pre-trimmed salad greens, pre-shredded cheese, canned chicken broth, and good-quality frozen rolls—subtle shortcuts that supplement those steps that must be done from scratch.

1 LASTLY, AND MOST IMPORTANT, BREATHE. Relax and enjoy the holidays. This is your special time with family and friends. Being together and loving each other is part of the joy of the season.